Praise for Live Like Lorelei

♥ ♥ ♥ ♥ ♥ ♥ ♥

The world would be a better place if we all learned to live like Lorelei...and Susan. That's why this book should be required reading—not just for medical parents or grievers or those wanting to support them —but for everyone who wants to understand what it means to live fully and bravely and beautifully.

— *Jessica Fein, author of Breath Taking*

A captivating story of embracing the lives we are given and the heartbreak we can't control. This is a wildly brave story to tell and it was hard to put down. An easy, but impactful, read. Suz's humble, witty, and raw retelling of her life-shifting journey into both motherhood and medical complexity is filled with grace, humor, and connection. You can't read this and not be impacted.

— *Carissa Robinson, MSW, Disability Advocate, Co-Founder of Coffin-Siris Syndrome Foundation*

Live Like Lorelei is nothing short of extraordinary. Suz writes with fearless honesty, deep wisdom, and a wit that will have you laughing through tears. Her humor is part of her magic—lightening even the heaviest moments and reminding us that joy can always be found, even in the hardest chapters of life.

In a world that often leans toward cynicism and despair, this book is a shining reminder that hope, courage, and love are still very much alive. While it speaks powerfully to families facing the realities of medical challenges, it's also for anyone ready to live more bravely, openly, and joyfully.

This is not just a memoir—it's a guide to becoming a bold, beautiful version of yourself, carried along by a voice that is as hilarious as it is inspiring. *Live Like Lorelei* deserves every one of its five stars.

— Alexa Fischer, Founder of Wishbeads,
Author, Speaker, Dreamer

This book broke my heart open and put it back together again. *Live Like Lorelei* captures the struggles of motherhood, the beauty of resilience, and the profound impact one little girl can leave on the world.

— Christi Rose, Caregiving Mama, Apricity
Hope Project Board of Directors

Suz has mastered the difficult art of holding two contrasting states to be true at once and not in conflict. *Live Like Lorelei* has heartbreak but also humor. The kind of heartbreak that leaves your heart open wider and able to hold more than you thought you could. The kind of humor that shows even the deepest darkness has bright light within it. Within the first sentences you'll have zero doubt you are hearing Suz's raw, true voice. And if this were not enough she concludes with practical tips for both those awash in grief and those that wish to be better support to them.

— Daniel DeFabio, Menkes Syndrome dad,
advocate and co-founder of The Disorder
Channel

Susan, you've brought normalcy to the lives we live as Medical Mamas, lives many others could never understand until, perhaps, now. You've found a way to highlight the beauty in medical parenthood without ignoring the hard work down in the trenches. *Live Like Lorelei* will be a guiding light for parents on this path.

— *Sarah Keller, Disability Advocate and*
Medical Mama

Susan's masterful storytelling in *Live Like Lorelei* has messages and takeaways for everyone, but the intimacy in which it gently pulls back the curtain on Lorelei's life and experiences gives medical and psychosocial professionals a raw and unabashed perspective on the challenges, strengths, and inherent wholeness of medical families. Hopefully, the Geoghegan's story will be etched on the hearts of all those caring for families navigating medically complex caregiving.

> — *Abigail Gellene-Beaudoin, Licensed Clinical Social Worker, Author of When Hope Changes and Our Baby Is Loved*

Live Like Lorelei clutches at your heart as it takes such sadness and turns it upward because Lorelei wasn't a little girl who would allow you to be sad. This book feels like you are sitting Susan having a conversation—real, vulnerable, deeply encouraging.

> — *Dr. Jenna Wheeler, Pediatric Critical Care*

Live Like Lorelei is filled with hope, despair, courage, and fear—and it reminds us that all of those feelings can exist in unison. Susan's words are a lifeline, reminding readers they are not failing, not broken, and not lost, even in the midst of chaos.

> — *Janice Belcher, Mito Mom*

Who knew a girl so little could impact a world so big. Susan's story took me on a real, genuine journey of holding onto joy even in the hardest of storms. May *Live Like Lorelei* remain a deep inspiration, a guiding and grounding light, that is etched and weaved into all of our future chapters, including the chapter where we one day cure FBXL4-Associated Mito-chondrial Disease!

> — *Dr. Keri-Lyn Kozul, FBXL4 Mitochondrial Disease Researcher*

From the moment I started listening to the *When Autumn Comes Podcast,* Suz felt like a friend. This book is no different. I found myself having to stop and really take in the profound truths that she is so generously sharing with us. She has gained so much wisdom through this heartbreaking and beautiful journey.

> — Katrina McElhinney, Medical Mama and Co-Hostess of *When Autumn Comes Podcast*

Wow! Just wow! I loved your sarcastic wit right out of the gate. I laughed and cried and will be thinking about the lessons of Lorelei's short but impactful life for a long time to come.

> — *Marnie Dyer, Parent Advocate, Apricity Hope Project Board of Directors*

Live Like Lorelei

Live Like Lorelei

A mother's story of finding herself through a little girl who was dying the day she was born.

Susan Benjaminson Geoghegan

HOPE FULL CO.
EST • 2021

Published by Hope Full Company

Virginia, USA

ISBN (paperback): 979-8-9999959-0-2

ISBN (ebook): 979-8-9999959-1-9

First Edition

Cover design by Susan B. Geoghegan

Interior design by Susan B. Geoghegan

Author photo by Leslie P. Bell

Author mother/daughter photo by Katie Wilson

This is a work of nonfiction. Some names and identifying details have been changed to protect privacy. The author is not a medical or legal professional, and the contents of this book are not intended as medical or legal advice.

Printed in the United States of America

For more information, visit: www.suzgeoghegan.com

For Benji.
May you always know that this book is as much
yours as it is your sister's—
that her story is woven into yours,
and both live forever in mine.

(And also because, let's be honest,
you deserve more than a footnote in your sister's book.)

Contents

Part Three

After Lorelei

Lorelei Elizabeth Geoghegan

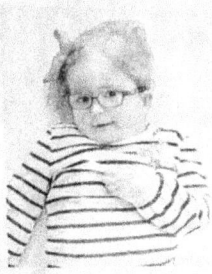

Lorelei "Doodle" Elizabeth Geoghegan, 5, of Suffolk, Virginia traded in her warrior princess cape and hair bow for the most beautiful angel wings on July 7, 2021. Lorelei faced battles every single day with hope in her heart, love in her eyes and perfect, epic hair. She accomplished more in her short five years than most could do in 100 years. Despite being nonverbal due to her rare form of Mitochondrial Disease, Lorelei shared her pure, yet often sassy, soul with everyone. She was an expert cuddler, lover of Disney movies, happy camper, hammock aficionado, sucker for fart noises, Daisy Girl Scout and guacamole lick-tester. Her heart was happiest when she was kicking, splashing, playing or floating in water. Lorelei leaves behind her proud, faithful, and dare we say exhausted Dada and Mama, Michael and Susan Geoghegan, her soulmate of a little brother, Benji, her companion dogs Olivia and Jovie Doodle - as well as loving grandparents, aunties and uncles. She powered through by the eternal grace of God, the never ending love of her family and the overwhelming support of her medical team and Fridays With Lorelei community. Lorelei's life will be celebrated on July 20, 2021 at 4PM at the Lesner Inn in Virginia Beach, VA. Dress code is bright colors, tie dye optional. In lieu of flowers, donations can be made to Lorelei and Benji's Fund for a Mito Cure (chop.donordrive.com/campaign/Lorelei), CHKD (secure.qgiv.com/for/chkd), Edmarc (www.edmarc.com) or SMILE (www.smileasier.org/donate) in her honor.

Please sign guestbook at obituaries.pilotonline.com

Foreword

On July 20, 2021, I stood before hundreds of people wearing a tie-dye dress. I had pink highlights in my wavy, curly hair, pinned back with a semi-gaudy pink bow that belonged to an incredibly sweet—albeit unapologetically sassy—little girl.

Two days prior, in the wee 4AM-ish hours when grief refused to let me sleep, I wrote the eulogy for my five-year-old daughter. And because all works of art deserve a title, I named it *Lessons from Lorelei*. Armed with waterproof mascara and her favorite bedtime book, I shared fifteen lessons I had learned from one of the most magical humans I have ever met.

After I finished her 20-minute eulogy, I was flooded with support and encouragement. Not because my daughter had died 13 days earlier—well, maybe that was part of it—but really, it was because her lessons resonated with every single person in that building. I was told that everyone left Lorelei's funeral feeling more hope, joy, and light than they had in a very long time. And not the usual kind of "light" people politely pretend to feel after a funeral, either. Most funerals leave folks feeling like Justin Timberlake's gray, joyless Troll before he discovered glitter and dance parties—but this one? People walked out glowing. Grief-stained, yes—but somehow lighter. Somehow more alive. Somehow more like Princess Poppy. (Perhaps it's worth noting: we danced to *Get Back Up Again* at Lorelei's funeral, so... this was not a normal funeral.)

And then everyone wanted a copy of Lorelei's life lessons.

At first, I thought I'd turn those 15 lessons into a little book. You know, something people might read on the toilet or leave on their coffee table as a conversation piece between stacks of unread mail and half-burned candles. But the more I wrote, the more I realized—there was so much more to the story. Fifteen lessons became a doorway, not a conclusion.

As a mom and a writer who never saw this plot twist coming, I learned more from my daughter than I could cram into a tidy bullet-point list. So I decided to take my time. To breathe. To bleed a little on these pages. To honor her story, and mine.

This is a memoir, which means it's my story—told through my memories, my perspective, my words. Lorelei's story is woven through mine, inseparable. And while my husband, Michael, my son, Benji, and others were there too, living their own versions, what you'll read here is how I carried it, how I remember it. Additionally, it is important to note that my perspective is that of a mother. I wasn't the one hooked up to monitors or lying in the hospital bed. I was the one at the bedside—interpreting, advocating, holding on—but also the one soaking up the giggles, the sparkle, the everyday magic that made her life more than her diagnosis.

Maybe you picked up this book because the cover caught your eye. Maybe you thought it was a synopsis of the seven seasons of *Gilmore Girls* (and honestly, respect). Maybe you're a fellow parent walking through the thick fog of mito-chondrial disease—or any other rare, brutal, and beautiful journey. Maybe you're here because you're looking for a story that reminds you there's still hope and softness in a hard world. Or maybe you accidentally downloaded the audio-book (gasp—if it ever exists, may I formally request Lauren Graham to narrate it?) and you have no clue how or why...

However you got here doesn't matter. What matters is that you're here. You're brave. And you are so, so loved. Thank you for being part of this story.

How to Live Like (Lorelei)

1. Do not take your calendar too seriously
2. Be outside as much as possible
3. Dance every day
4. Communication comes in all forms.
5. A hammock is never, ever a bad idea.
6. You do not have to say or do a lot, or even leave your house to make an impact
7. Do not take life too seriously. None of us make it out alive.
8. Water. Is. Life.
9. Embrace what you are handed.
10. Make a list.
11. Compliment people and let them know they are loved.
12. You do not have to eat everything that is put in front of you.
13. When things get hard, look up.
14. It is okay to be rare and different.
15. Read before bed.

 Mama misses you Doodle.

Prologue

The Princess Captain and her Mama

Once upon a time, there was a young princess named Lorelei. She had beautiful strawberry blonde hair, the heart of a warrior, and the nonchalant sense of humor that most comedians spend years trying to master on the improv stage. She lived a life tucked away in a tower, hidden from most of the people who adored her. But somehow, she still had this mystical ability to radiate her love to them, no matter how far away they were. She lived a simple, yet enormous life. A life full of color, adventures, and stubborn joy. She believed in magic, hope, and light, even though she spent most of her days just trying to survive.

Okay, full disclosure: she wasn't technically a real-life princess like the ones at Disney World. Because if she were, that would make me a queen, and I am nowhere near that. I'm more like a sea captain who's been tossed around in more storms than she ever signed up for. My old wooden ship is tattered, worn down, and sagging like a 40-year-old mama who spent too much time with a breast pump. My sails are patched with neon pink duct tape. I'm surviving on rum and grief pie, which I'm fairly certain queens don't eat. Or if they do, they definitely don't admit it. Either way, I'm more of a foul-mouthed exhausted pirate than some poised monarch with a crown and a skincare routine.

But here's the twist. I am Mama. Lorelei's Mama. And as much as I wanted to believe I was running this tight ship-wreck, she was the one at the helm. She was the Princess Captain. I was just lucky enough to be her first mate.

I had the privilege of being her voice during her journey with mitochondrial disease. She didn't have words, so I wrote for her. She couldn't sit up, so she leaned on me. Not enough muscle tone to walk? You better believe I got a little stronger carrying her 42-pound body up and down the stairs. And making her voice heard every step of the way. (Unfortunately, I'm still not skinny, thanks to the aforementioned grief pie.)

Lorelei may have physically left this world, but somehow, she handed me the compass on her way out. The story she lived—and the way she lived it—didn't disappear when she did. It cracked me wide open. It forced me to confront parts of myself I had long ignored. It's reshaped the way I move through this life. And now I'm trying to *Live Like Lorelei*. It's messy. It's imperfect. It's not always pretty. But it's real.

I'll be your tour guide through this book. Not only of the chapters Lorelei inspired during her five-ish short years on Earth, but of the ones that came before her and after her too.

Lorelei was a soul and a spirit we should all learn from. If the world practiced even a little of her gumption and love, it would be a softer, braver place.

But this isn't just her story.

It's mine too.

Because grief didn't end my journey. It rerouted it.

So grab a drink and a slice of key lime pie, and let's do this.

With hope and stubborn joy —

Lorelei + Benji's Mama,

SUZ

♡

Part One

Before Lorelei

These chapters hold the girl I once was—her stories still soft around the edges, color-coded pages filling with hope, unaware that the plot was about to twist. She didn't yet know the storm would rewrite her, shaping the mother and woman she was always meant to become.

Chapter 1

Mitochondria and Muumuus

...strangely, not as unrelated as they sound.

Before I carried grief in my bones and Do Not Resuscitate letters in my purse, I carried a clipboard and glitter while wearing sensible shoes at weddings.

Literally and metaphorically, I have always been the planner. The box-checker. The girl who believed that if you did everything right—if you played nice, worked hard, showed up early, invited everyone to your party, and followed the rules—you'd be rewarded with a good, full, happy life.

This border-collie-esque level of control started early. I'm sure my parents could tell you (with a touch of trauma in their voices) about the many musical productions I choreographed to *NSYNC hits. My sister and I performed in our pajamas, jumping off the brick hearth, skinning our knees as we slid across the Berber carpet for the grand finale while my dad tried to watch *Cheers* on the television screen that was directly behind us.

I have zero dance skills, but that did not stop me. It was loud and awkward, but you are correct to assume that we hit every mark. Looking back, I realize not every kid needs therapy because their older sister turned the living room into a Broadway stage—but every adult I know is still choreographing, trying to make their chaos look less like a mess and more like a masterpiece.

Planning made my soul happy. It gave me a sense of purpose and, maybe more importantly, a sense of control. It also seemed to make the people around me happy, or at least entertained. And I liked that feeling. I liked knowing what to expect. I liked being in charge.

In elementary school, I hosted entire carnivals in our backyard for the neighborhood kids. I wish I could say it only happened once, on some dewy spring afternoon, but truthfully this was a repeat offense. I would spend days preparing cardboard booths and hanging signs that made everything look official. There were handmade tickets, small prizes, and invitations carefully written out like it was an actual community event, not just some Tuesday in suburbia.

Other kids played pretend. I scheduled it.

It is only now, after decades of life and thousands of dollars in therapy, that I'm realizing planning and control have a very symbiotic relationship. Planning wasn't just about organizing logistics or making things pretty with a glitter pen and a timeline. It was about safety. It was about trying to prevent the worst from happening by staying five steps ahead of it.

If I could plan it, I could control it. If I could control it, maybe I wouldn't get hurt. Maybe no one would get hurt.

Control gave—scratch that. Control continues to give me a false sense of peace. A temporary stillness in the chaos of "what ifs." That is how my brain has always worked. I like control. I like when things make sense. I like planning things and watching them unfold exactly the way I envision. I thought life was something you could organize if you were good enough. If you followed the rules. If you earned it. That belief stuck with me. And as I grew up, I got very good at checking the boxes.

☑ Do well in school? Learn an instrument! *Check. Check!*

☑ Volunteer hours? Hello, opossum-cuddling-on-the-trail at the Virginia Aquarium. *Check!*

☑ Church, leadership, scouts, extracurriculars, learn a foreign language? *Check and Guten Tag!*

I was a professional box-checker before I could drive.

It wasn't just about getting things done—it was about getting them *right*. I didn't want a gold star. I wanted the whole damn sticker chart. I wanted things to be beautiful and impressive and exactly as they were supposed to be. That is probably why my 10th-grade science project sat on the top shelf of my closet for fifteen years before my mom finally threw it away.

The assignment was to build a 3D model of a cell for biology class. Most kids either brought in basic diagrams that had been glued together at the breakfast table or a cake with candy representing the internal structure of a cell—minus the bite their dad stole. Not me. I had plans. I had a vision. I wasn't going to slap together a diagram. I was going to make something spectacular.

At midnight, I was on the kitchen floor, surrounded by styrofoam balls, paint, glitter, and the kind of tears that flow from perfectionist panic. I needed a mitochondria that looked Pinterest-worthy before Pinterest even existed. I needed the nucleus to shine. I needed every part of that cell to be flawless. Hours later, I was sleep-deprived and emotionally fragile, worrying over endoplasmic reticulum, but the project was complete and it was beautiful.

Ironically, I created a perfect cell.

I didn't know how that word—*mitochondria*—would one day knock the breath out of me in a quiet Neonatal Intensive Care Unit (NICU) conference room. Back then, it was just homework. A grade. An assignment to check off the syllabus. A chance to do something excellent. My mind should have thought of a million different things when they told me my daughter had a rare disease. But when they said Mitochondrial Disease and her name in the same sentence, I immediately went back to my perfectly created, meticulously labeled, glitter-covered styrofoam cell.

JUST AS MY PARENTS, teachers, and guidance counselors told me to do, I studied hard and got into James Madison University, my dream college, because people were kind and they held doors open for each other. Despite all of my planning, I had no idea what I wanted to be when I grew up, but found my way in Communication Studies with a focus on Organizational Communication and a minor in Marketing. I was good at organizing, so it made sense that I could help organizations streamline their workflows and communicate efficiently. Communication Studies was a smart, flexible choice. I liked people. I liked words. I liked the idea of helping things make sense.

Shocker: I was not the typical college kid. I studied hard and followed all the rules. I did not party much. The epitome of my time in college was when my then-roommates-now-best-friends and I found ourselves walking down Main Street on the way to a Halloween party dressed as The Golden Girls. Other girls were stumbling past us dressed as sexy cats and naughty nurses, while we were rocking bouffant hair and muumuus, passing cheesecake out to everyone at the party. Most of my peers looked like they were auditioning to be the next MTV host. My roommates and I looked like your grandmother's bridge club. We didn't try to make it hot or rebellious. We followed the rules. We made it hilarious. And we had the best time ever.

After graduation, I landed a great job in sales and ranked fourth nationally in that company. (Ahem, gold star!) I traveled. I did mission work in third-world countries. I bought my first house. And I finally got the red Jeep Wrangler I'd dreamed of since I was a little girl—the one I used to picture myself driving with the top down, my hair blowing behind me like Barbie in a shampoo commercial. I had not found my future husband yet, but everything else seemed to be falling into place. I was working hard and I was living the dream.

Because apparently having one full-time job wasn't

enough, I decided to start my own business. Despite not having professional experience, I had decades of hands-on training, so I opened my own wedding and event planning company. My first bride hired me, no questions asked, and no portfolio to show her. I called my company 29:11 *Celebrations*. I quickly picked up more and more clients. I was so good at planning, people were literally paying me to do it for them.

When I was naming my business, I knew two things. First, I wanted it to reflect me and where I was at that point in my life. And second, I wanted it to start with a number or the letter A so that it appeared early in the search engines (read: at the time, the phone book!).

The name came from Jeremiah 29:11. That verse had always meant something to me. *"For I know the plans I have for you,"* declares the Lord. *"Plans to prosper you and not to harm you, plans to give you hope and a future."*

Every client would ask me where the number came from, and I would explain to them that we could plan every single detail of their wedding day, but in the end none of us can control if it's going to storm. I told them I could plan to the best of my ability, but things would always happen the way they were supposed to happen.

I believed it.

To my core.

Sort of.

I guess I thought I believed it?

Okay, I believed-ish.

I knew it, but perhaps I didn't fully grasp that sometimes

the plan includes the storm—not the kind that merely dampens a wedding day, but the kind that can upend your entire world.

College Golden Girl
Halloween 2005

Chapter 2

First Comes Love, Then Comes Marriage

...and then comes a baby in the— grandma's attic?

efore he had a name, he was just *"Guam Guy."* That's what my friends and I called him because I had met him online one week before he was stationed in Guam. This was before swiping left or right was a thing. But it was well after the "if you like pina coladas" style personal ads. We met on a dating site that somehow involved fishing, but not the kind of fishing I thought it was.

He emailed me first, and when I read that he was in the military, I did not reply. Nothing against the military—thank you for your service—but I was a local Hampton Roads, Virginia girl who lived surrounded by military bases with no military family to speak of. I watched school friends move all over the world. I wanted to feel safe and secure. I didn't want to relocate. I wanted to feel home.

When I did not reply, he emailed again asking, "What kind of bike do you like to ride?" In hindsight—what?? But I replied because that meant he actually looked at my pictures and I was deep into my road cycling phase at the time. That phase didn't last too long, but the relationship did.

Despite his bleak, one liner email about my bicycle, he actually wrote great emails, with complete words and decent grammar, which was rare in the world of online dating. He shared YouTube links of songs he liked and clips from shows we could both laugh at from opposite sides of the globe. We clicked as much as two people can click virtually (pun intended) without phone calls or video messaging. For four months, our entire relationship grew and existed in a *You've Got Mail* movie style, complete with a fourteen-hour time difference and no guarantee that this wasn't a beautifully worded scam.

When he finally came home, I worried the connection we'd built through a screen might not survive the real world— or that something as simple as bad chemistry (or bad smell) would end us. But he turned out to be even better in person. Steady. Sincere. Protective. The kind of guy who reads every sign in a museum and fixes things without YouTube. I was smitten. And "Guam Guy" officially became Michael.

We did everything right, just like we were supposed to. A rooftop engagement. A wedding where no detail went unlooked. Guests left covered in glitter. (Author's note: This is not a metaphor. Do not use glitter tulle as table runners.) The story was unfolding. It was perfect and it was ours.

After the honeymoon, we traveled, tackled home projects, and dabbled at being grown-ups with a joint Costco membership. We lived in the house he had bought before we met, and together we worked to make it ours. At one point I decided it *needed* a screen porch—the kind with fairy lights and cozy furniture where I could sip wine and romanticize life. The kind where I would be able to watch our future kids play in the backyard. But when the quote came in at the same price as a down payment on a new house, things escalated quickly...

We did what any two ambitious, slightly naive, spread-sheet-obsessed people do: we sold our house and decided to build our dream home instead. To save money during construction, we moved into my grandmother's attic, which, in hindsight, I cannot recommend. Especially if there's any possibility that you're pregnant.

My mom was our realtor. My dad was our builder. Michael was the engineer. And I, naturally, was the planner with vision boards, a newfound obsession with tile patterns, and Pottery Barn dreams on a Walmart budget. Our new house was going to be perfect. We'd build a home. We'd build a life.

That was the plan, anyway.

♥♥♥♥♥♥♥

I AM someone who thrives when sunlight pours through big open windows, so living in my grandmother's attic took a toll on my mental health. It's amazing how the spaces we live in seep into us. A house can lift you up or press down on your chest like a too-low ceiling.

Dark paneling, slanted ceilings, a tiny window with an AC unit blocking any light that should be trickling in. The cave-like atmosphere made me feel like I was living in the Batcave, with my hard-of-hearing Nana downstairs blasting

Fox News around the clock. Hardly the backdrop for a love story.

Less than a month after moving into the cave, Michael was away for military training. I woke up to a voice. Not in my head, but also not out loud. Deep, calm, and firm. I heard, "You are pregnant."

I calmly sat up in bed and looked around, trying to figure out if this was coming from the television downstairs. And then I heard it again.

Now, this may be TMI, but it's my memoir, so here goes nothing: we had tried to get pregnant one time. One. And not in a "this is totally going to work" way. More like, "this better not happen on the first try or we will be living with Nana and have to put the baby in a drawer until our house is built" kind of way.

So when I heard that voice, I sat straight up in the dark cave-like-attic, grabbed a pregnancy test, sprinted to the bathroom and sure enough: positive.

I texted Michael immediately.

Me: *Call me.*

Michael: *In a training. You okay?*

Me: *It's an emergency.*

Two minutes later, my phone rang.

I told him the news, a little breathless, a little panicked. And his response?

"This is not an emergency. I'll call you later."

Which, to be fair, I think he meant it in the "you're safe, everything is okay" kind of way. But it was not the cinematic reaction I'd imagined. And yet, somehow, it was perfect for us. Understated. Surprising. Slightly ridiculous. In a cave.

That voice I heard, the one that told me I was pregnant, turned out to be something I would come to know well. It was not just a fluke. It was a guide. A compass. A quiet whisper that stayed with me throughout my daughter's entire life.

She was meant to be here.

She was meant to be mine.

♥ ♥ ♥ ♥ ♥ ♥ ♥

Pregnancy announcement on the job site of our new house in 2015

Wedding day 2013 — they had no clue what was coming...

Chapter 3

CoverGirl

...the easy, breezy, beautiful chapter.

I remember exactly where I was when the phone rang: walking past the makeup aisle in Target. I was on my way to give them all my money and head home when my phone buzzed deep in my purse. A couple of weeks earlier, I did the standard lab work offered to expecting mothers to make sure nothing is "wrong" with the baby. The one that screens for "basic" genetic conditions like Down Syndrome. Not rare diseases. Certainly not Mitochondrial Disease.

After the nurse had drawn my blood, she explained that they would call me within seven business days with the results. Seven days came and went, and I didn't worry. I was so confident that my baby was healthy, I did not give it a second thought. Oh, sweet and innocent Suz.

Then came that moment. I was mindlessly stopped in my tracks on the CoverGirl aisle, surrounded by 50 shades of pink, and now contemplating whether I needed another mascara, as the nurse greeted me on the call:

"Mrs. Geoghegan? This is the nurse from *I love you, dear reader, but I'm not telling you who my doctor is*. Can you confirm your birthday?" she asked politely.

Even before I became a medical mom, I would always joke, "Wouldn't it be more identifiable if I spelled my last name correctly instead of giving my birthday? Anyone can look that up, but very few can spell Geoghegan, let alone pronounce it correctly."

Crickets.

I gave her my birthday.

She replied, in a perfectly pleasant, matter-of-fact tone, "I'm calling to tell you your blood work came back fine. Looks like a healthy baby!"

I thanked her, hung up the phone... and paused.

It's funny what our brains choose to remember. I couldn't tell you what I had for dinner last week, but I remember the time of day, where I was standing, and the purse I was carrying when I received *that* call. I remember the way the fluorescent lights buzzed and how I was holding a tube of lip gloss. And I remember the thought that followed the call so vividly it still stings.

Of course the baby is healthy, I thought. *God wouldn't give me a sick child.*

Even now, anxiety churns and scratches like rusty barbed wire on a chalkboard in my chest as I write that sentence.

God would not give me a sick child.

I can proudly say I've come a long, long way since that version of me. But if New Me could travel back to that CoverGirl moment and whisper a few things into Old Me's ear, I would.

Who in the world do you think you are?

That's what I want to ask her... but not with judgment. Because that belief she holds? It's what she knows. It is written into her bones, stitched into the way she sees the world. And nothing, not even this fictional conversation across decades of time, could prepare her for what is coming. So yes, my sarcastic tone might land like a slap. It might feel abrupt or unkind. But still, with heartbreak, with grace, with the ache of knowing what's ahead, I want to take her by the shoulders, look her in the eyes and say:

"Who in the world do you think you are?

Sweet girl, you think you can earn a future. You believe that if you do A plus B, you'll get C—because that's how it's supposed to work. But sometimes A plus B equals FBXL4.

You cannot craft a predictable life with your goodness. You cannot control it with your color-coded planner. You cannot earn it with gold stars.

And what's coming? You didn't earn that either. Nor do you deserve it.

No one earns suffering. Just like no one earns joy or safety or ease. Grief doesn't come to the wicked, and comfort doesn't only land on the righteous.

Unfortunately, that's not how any of this works.

It is going to be okay. Not because your story turns out how you want it. But because you will learn to write a new story. Now turn around and remember this: grief and joy, imperfection and beauty, can—and will—absolutely sit side by side. Also, buy the foundation that includes SPF. And for the love of God, go take a nap. You're going to need it."

Was the belief of "deserving" mine or was it something

the world handed me, wrapped in glittery faith and graphically pleasing quotes? The universe doesn't keep score. Some babies are born sick and some mothers break in half and still show up. Sometimes faith is just sitting in the unknown, saying, I will stay.

Because here's the truth: I did not earn my daughter, and later my son's, health. I did not deserve their diagnosis either.

It took me years to unlearn that. Years to unravel the quiet promise I thought I had secured, that good girls get good outcomes.

I didn't know it yet, but the version of myself who stood there, innocent and smug, naive and hopeful, next to the CoverGirl display was about to be shattered. Not all at once. Not even quickly. But little by little, my grip on the myth of certainty through planning would loosen. And in its place, I would slowly learn how to hold profound grief and unending joy in the same hand.

That moment in the CoverGirl aisle was the first crack for that version of me. A version that I still honor, even now, because she is part of this story too. She was living the easy, breezy and beautiful chapter. Now, years later, I can't walk past that makeup aisle without feeling it all: the ache of innocence lost, the bitterness of hindsight, and the tinge of a life less heavy that still lives somewhere in my core.

Chapter 4

The Mag Drip at the End of the Tunnel

...when the warning signs are also rescue signs.

My pregnancy was shockingly normal, despite my not-so-normal living situation. My grandmother would walk through the room while I was sitting at her dining table, my makeshift desk, and gently pat my belly as if it were a baby, while I was on calls with the president of my largest, national marketing client. I met contractors on the jobsite, weaving my belly through our newly-framed, work-in-progress home. I drove forty-five minutes, give-or-take traffic, to get to my OBGYN office, because finding a new doctor seemed silly if we didn't even have a hometown to call our home base.

The irony, of course, is that my semi-perfect pregnancy boiled down to two very serious concerns: saving the planet one cloth diaper at a time, and surviving the Hampton Roads Bridge Tunnel. Since we had moved, as the locals say, "across the water," I was absolutely convinced I would go into labor during rush-hour and end up birthing a child in the smoggy depths of the tunnel while a container ship motored overhead. But life had far bigger worries waiting for us on the eve of 32 weeks.

The Monday following my baby shower and Super Bowl 50, I woke up unable to bend my fingers. I had heard it was normal to feel more bloated in the third trimester, and my ankles were swollen from a busy weekend of shindigging, so I chalked it up to the usual pregnancy things. After Nana's all-day nagging, I finally called my doctor to mention the swelling. I figured they'd tell me to prop up my feet and drink some water. Instead, they told me to come in immediately.

Bless the nurse who checked my blood pressure that day. She took it twice, then went to grab a new cuff, checked two more times, and finally said she needed to get a second opinion. Something wasn't right. A nurse supervisor came in, followed by the doctor, each one confirming the reading.

My blood pressure was 175/120. Which is pretty impressive if we were talking bowling scores, but about 50 points higher than anyone wants while growing a human.

"You're not going back to the attic," the doctor said. "You're going to the hospital. Now."

Cue total panic. And a magnesium drip.

They maxed it out. Forty hours on IV magnesium sulfate to bring my blood pressure down. This was the upper limit of what's typically considered safe. In a dim, cozy-in-a-sterile-kinda-way hospital room, they worked to stabilize me—not necessarily the baby—because at that point, everyone still thought she was fine. I was told we'd be in the hospital for the next eight weeks to let Lorelei keep baking while they monitored my preeclampsia. Not ideal at all, but once my blood pressure stabilized, I figured it was better than the bat cave I had been living in.

Only... it wasn't just my body that needed saving.

♥♥♥♥♥♥♥

ONCE MY VITALS LEVELED OUT, they began to realize Lorelei was not okay. Her heart rate was dipping and her vitals were slow to stabilize. Something wasn't right and every medical professional around me seemed to be on high alert.

I still believe, with my whole being, that God and that deep calm, guardian angel voice I heard in the attic, used my high blood pressure to get Lorelei safely into a hospital. Because on the day she was born, she was dying—and we had no idea.

It was a cold, rainy, icy February day and the hospital rotation doctor turned out to be my doctor—the same one who had sent me there days before. She's the person who walked me through making the first big medical decision on behalf of my child. She explained that, because of Lorelei's needs, I needed to be transferred to Norfolk General—a hospital back on the other side of the water, directly connected to the Level IV NICU at the Children's Hospital of The King's Daughters. That transfer would ensure Lorelei had immediate access to the highest level of care after delivery.

To this day, I still see that OB at my annual appointments. I thank her every single time. She was the person who was with me when this started, and her care, compassion and concern saved my daughter's life before we even knew it needed saving. Her actions gifted me time... with Lorelei.

On that snowy Monday evening (author's note: half an inch of snow in Coastal Virginia is typically considered a State of Emergency) I was loaded into my very first ambulance ride, and back across the bridge tunnel we went. As folks tailgated and zoomed past us on the bridge, I couldn't help but sit there with the silly feeling that I had been so worried about this tunnel (and cloth diapers). And here I was, navigating traffic from the back of an ambulance on slick roads, transferring to a hospital that I had not planned for. I had not researched it. I was not ready. All I knew about the children's hospital was its reputation: the place for the sickest kids, the one my community had fundraised for my entire life. It wasn't supposed to happen this way.

When we arrived at Norfolk General, the team there was far less concerned. They told us the previous hospital had overreacted. After getting situated and hooking me up to all the machines they said Lorelei was stable. They said she looked good. They told me I would likely be there for several more weeks. And I finally exhaled.

Michael went home for the first time in a week to sleep that night and my mom took his place at my bedside. Next door, my hospital neighbors were throwing a full-blown baby shower. Every cousin, friend, and co-worker they had ever met must have come to celebrate at 10PM on a weekday. Sounds of joy and chaos poured through our shared bathroom. Meanwhile my room was dim and unnervingly quiet. I turned on *The Bachelor,* let the reality television drama numb my nerves, and I began to believe that this would be my reality for the next six weeks.

As the Bachelor began handing out his roses and my neighbors continued to party, my new doctor came in to introduce herself. She was calm, warm, attentive, and looked like a 12-year-old. Miss *Doogie Howser, MD* had to climb onto a step stool to examine me in bed. She asked what I was thinking and how I was holding up with everything happening. I vulnerably said, "I'm exhausted. I'm afraid if I let my guard down and fall asleep someone's going to come in, wake me up and tell me we have to deliver the baby."

She smiled kindly and assured me, "No, she's stable. We won't do that. *I promise.* Now get some rest."

Five hours later, I woke up to her step stool creaking as she stood over me and said "So... I lied."

Lorelei was crashing, and no one understood why. It was time to pull her from the game. It was time for a trip to the Operating Room. But we had phone calls to make: Michael, the doula, the Level IV NICU next door...

When Michael, who had finally fallen asleep for the first time in days, answered the phone at 3AM, my mom and I could tell he wasn't okay. Considering his quick response to my pregnancy announcement, the poor guy had a full blown panic attack when it was an actual emergency. Thank goodness for our doula, Lacey. Despite the pivot to a c-section, she made it in time and became my support stand-in when Michael nearly fainted putting on surgery scrubs. Neither Michael nor I saw Lorelei as she was born. Neither of us held her. But at 4AM on February 16, 2016 I heard a raspy, unexpected squeaky cry when she was pulled out of my womb. And it was enough to give me hope.

♥♥♥♥♥♥♥

LORELEI WAS TINY. Under three pounds. Below the third percentile for a 33-weeker. Her skin was pale, almost gray—not the plump pink you picture when you think of newborns. A fine layer of lanugo, that soft downy "fur" preemies wear like an unfinished coat, clung to her entire body. She had a face only a mother could love, but in reality, she looked like a damp subway rat who missed the last train home. I had never seen a baby so scrawny before. But she was breathing on her own. And after I got the briefest glimpse of her, she went straight to the special care NICU, while I was sent to the Post-Anesthesia Care Unit to recover.

Hours passed, and I was taken to my room on the mother-baby floor. Except, I didn't have my baby. I still had not truly seen her. I hadn't held her. And I didn't even know if she was okay. I could hear visitors happily popping in for all the new mommies in the rooms around me, while the air in my room was so crisp and quiet with worry.

Mid-afternoon, still with zero updates, a nurse popped by to check on my incision, unaware that I was completely in the dark about everything happening to my baby. My mom took her new grandma duties very seriously and demanded an update on Lorelei, proclaiming, "She is a brand new mom and hasn't even seen her baby. It has been over twelve hours since delivery!"

The nurse's face went white as she said, "I thought you

knew. They're transferring her to the children's hospital. Now."

Somewhere in my post-magnesium, post-operation, post-birth, post-all-the-planned-things-out-the-window phases, I remember this nurse saying, "Screw it. Get in the wheelchair!" and we blasted down the mother-baby hallway at a speed that felt like a rocket ship. Yes, I was high on pain medication but I very clearly remember what transpired next as we flew into the special care NICU:

Nurse (probably sweating, running a 4-minute mile): MOM TAKE YOUR SHIRT OFF! DAD SCRUB IN!

Me (head spinning like I just got off the Gravitron in 1997, awkwardly removing my shirt like I was about to do a dizzy strip show): Uh, okay...

My nurse (still yelling): Don't you put that baby in that transport isolette yet!

Another nurse: This is against the rules. You cannot do this!

My nurse (to a different nurse): GET A CAMERA!

Rule-following nurse: YOU CANNOT DO THIS! STOP!

My nurse: HERE SHE COMES, MOM!

And then—five seconds of rebellion.

Time collapsed into those five stolen seconds. Lorelei was curled to my chest, impossibly small. My hand timidly spanned her like a giant cupping something fragile. Her ribs rose and fell beneath my palm; she was light as a baby bird settling into her mama's nest. Around us, alarms and orders blurred to static; the only sound I noticed was the hush of her breath against my skin. That newborn sweetness—warm and pure—grounding me in a way the morphine haze couldn't touch. My head was spinning but my eyes didn't leave her. I traced the curve of her tiny arm with one finger, memorizing her shape, setting her into memory as though I could stop the clock forever.

And just like that—the spell broke. Frantic voices crashed in, snapping me back into fluorescent reality.

Photographer nurse: I got a picture!

Transport team: She has to go NOW!

Rule-following nurse: You will get reported for this.

My nurse (gently): You okay, Mom? She's in good hands now. Did you feel her on your chest? Don't listen to her... sometimes we have to break the rules. Let's get you back to your room.

And then they took my baby away. I was wheeled down a hallway, past all the other moms holding their newborns, as guests happily poured in with balloons and sushi. I was scared and confused, and no one was celebrating in my room.

That moment rewrote me.

I thought I had time. I thought I had a plan. But it turns out, I had five quick seconds.

Because life rarely gives you notice when it's about to rewrite your entire story.

From the very beginning, Lorelei broke the rules and left me dazed and confused in her wake. She arrived on her own terms, careless of my plans, writing her own story.

It wouldn't be the last time I had to let go of what I thought our future should look like. This was going to be the kind of story we survived, together.

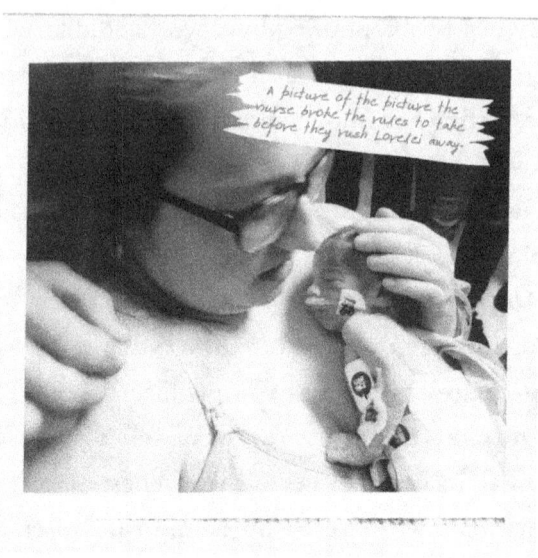

Part Two

With Lorelei

These pages hold the becoming of a mother—tossed by waves, yes, but also fueled by middle-of-the-night hospital coffee, holding grief in one hand and joy in the other, and learning that hope can anchor you even when the ground keeps shifting.

Chapter 5

When a Chaplain and a Geneticist Walk into a Bar

...and by bar, I mean hospital room.

I expected banners and streamers. A parade. Fanfare shouting, *"Huzzah! Welcome to Motherhood!"*

But just as Emily Perl Kingsley's essay suggests, we had spent our lives planning parenthood as if it was a vacation to Italy—savoring visions of gelato and authentic pasta. Instead, our plane landed in Holland, where the solemn "Welcome to Holland" committee awaited us, noticeably lacking in Dutch snacks or comforting smiles. There were no matching hospital outfits in artsy black-and-white photos. No "I'm new here!" onesies. No family waiting with balloons. Just fluorescent lights, confusion, and the kind of anxiety that hums under the surface like faulty wiring on the verge of sparking a disaster.

There was no joy and very little hope. Just a blur of exhaustion, depression, and sterile hospital air. And my baby, Lorelei, bewildering the doctors and struggling to survive.

What they first called a "typical preemie adjustment"

unraveled within hours into something terrifying. She was crashing, and she was crashing fast.

Lorelei had been transferred from the main hospital where I delivered her to the children's hospital next door. Thankfully, my brilliant doctor had listened to some sort of guiding voice and transferred me by ambulance less than twenty-four hours before delivery. If she hadn't, my unstable baby would have been transferred forty-five minutes away from me by ambulance. Instead, she was just next door.

Despite the short distance, I felt like Lorelei had been dropped in Holland to fight for her life in the NICU, while I was stuck in Italy, recovering from a C-section in the overly cheerful mommy-baby wing. And it had all started back in the United States, where I thought we were just preparing for a normal birth. It was a whirlwind tour of confusion, chaos, and fear.

And then a chaplain and a geneticist walked into my hospital room.

No, really. They did.

I was in bed, stitched up and stunned, when they appeared with clipboards and concerned faces, asking questions about resuscitation preferences, quality of life, and genetic history. I blinked at them through the haze of pain meds and trauma and thought, *Is this some kind of joke? And no, my husband and I are not each other's cousins.*

Because let's be clear: when a chaplain and a geneticist walk into your hospital room, it isn't a joke. There is no punchline. It is an epic plot twist, one that shows up at the beginning of a very different story than the one you thought you were creating.

I didn't know it then, but those two people would become part of our lives in ways I never imagined. They were there at the beginning, they continued to show up throughout the middle, and five years later, they would both be in the room again when Lorelei took her last breath.

In the first 24 hours of life, Lorelei was already drawing people in and building her village. She radiated something even then—something magnetic. A quiet kind of magic, or maybe a need that vibrated so deeply it reached people before words ever would. There was always someone. The right nurse. The right doctor. The chaplain who held space. The geneticist who wouldn't stop searching for answers.

I used to think it was just luck. That maybe Lorelei was the one pulling magical strings. But now, years removed, I can see it more clearly. As I sit here telling her story—*my* story—I realize something I never used to believe.

God always sends the right people. And at the exact right time.

I didn't see it in the moment. Most of my years as a caregiver, I felt abandoned, scared, and alone—but *especially* in the beginning. Those early days felt like being dropped into a storm without a compass, or Holland without a GPS. But looking back now, the pattern is undeniable. Lorelei built her village... and maybe, just maybe, I was being given mine too.

AFTER MICHAEL and I confirmed we were definitely not distant cousins, full genome sequencing—a blood test that analyzes nearly every gene in the body to detect mutations—

was ordered. No one had to say it out loud, it was clear: everyone was baffled by my daughter.

The NICU team ran test after test and kept her as stable as possible. Her ammonia levels were at an unsurvivable high, and her lactic acid was consistently elevated higher than a marathon runner at the end of the race. Paired with a grade-four brain bleed, among other things common for tiny preemies, her symptoms didn't match any single diagnosis. And yet, her body was failing.

My baby was dying and I didn't even feel like a mom yet. I hadn't held her. I hadn't fed her. I had barely touched her. She was behind glass, covered in wires and tubes, and I had to ask permission to lay a finger on her tiny body.

On day seven, I was finally allowed to change her diaper. I was absurdly proud. This was the first diaper I had ever changed in my life. Yes, I lived thirty-one years before changing a single diaper. My lack of motherly experience shined through when the nurse laughed as she informed me that I put the diaper on Lorelei backwards. Some moments mark your entrance into motherhood not with joy—but with humility. This was one of those moments.

It took nine days before it was safe enough for me to finally hold my child. Nine days before I felt like she was even mine and not a puppy I had to leave at the pound. Cradling Lorelei helped the fog begin to part, just enough for a little light to filter in—warmth creeping into the haze like sunshine in winter. Love nestling in gently beside the grief.

They called her a "feed and grower." They said she just needed calories and time. One nurse even assured me, with callous confidence, that Lorelei would be home by her due date. I remember a bedside conversation with a perplexed doctor who said, "Maybe—just maybe—she really is just a preemie. Because none of this makes sense."

I joined preemie NICU groups on Facebook, trying to find community. Trying to understand. Trying to feel less alone. Trying to feel seen as a mom on a path I never meant to take. But I didn't find my people there.

Because Lorelei wasn't *just* a preemie. And I wasn't *just* a new mom.

♥♥♥♥♥♥♥

In TRUE LORELEI FASHION, always one for dramatic timing and holiday interruptions, diagnosis day arrived right on theme.

February 29, 2016.

Leap Day.

Which also happens to be an internationally observed day called Rare Disease Day. The rarest day of the entire year.

Lorelei was thirteen days old when we were called into a windowless conference room that smelled like stale coffee and despair. Two brand-new bewildered parents sat across from the head neonatologist, lead geneticist, a social worker, a chaplain, and a few residents who looked like they were on the edge of their seats—ready to learn how to deliver bad news.

Science (and the doctors who sat in front of me as I bewilderedly glanced around a room of serious faces) said that Lorelei had FBXL4 Mitochondrial Disease (Mito). As they confirmed it was ultra-rare, complex, and life-limiting, the world around me seemed to spin in circles and pause at the same exact time.

That was the day we joined a club no one wants to be part of. That was the day the story split—*Before Diagnosis* and *After.*

We all have a moment when the story we thought we were living disappears, and a new one begins.

That was the day I became a medical mom.

A mom who would learn to fake it until she made it. Until we made it.

A mom who would cry in hospital bathrooms when no one was listening.

A mom who would face a heartache most people could never comprehend.

A mom who would experience the purest form of love, from children who didn't need words to say "I love you."

That was the day the life I planned and worked so hard for imploded. The dream was gone. But the girl was here. And she was everything.

I grieved the future I thought I was due. But I chose the girl—Lorelei, and the girl I was becoming. And I would choose us again and again.

♥♥♥♥♥♥♥

Holding hands for the first time. Look at her tiny knee under my binkie finger...

First time really holding her, when she was nine days old.

Chapter 6

Powerhouse

...the cellular function of an unstoppable spirit.

This isn't a story about mitochondrial disease.

It's a story about a girl who was pure magic. It's a story about a girl whose laugh came from her belly and her feisty spirit came from her strawberry blonde hair. It's a story about a girl who changed me from the person I was *before her*, to the person I am *because of her*.

But to understand our story—to truly understand why even the simplest moments were so hard-fought and holy—you need to understand the disease Lorelei was up against.

She was thirteen days old when I first heard the words "FBXL4 Mitochondrial Disease."

Michael and I were sitting in a solemn conference room with too many specialists and too few answers. The doctors spoke calmly, clinically. I heard them say words like *"progressive," "neurological," "life-limiting,"* but I couldn't comprehend them. The words, delivered with very little hope, bounced off of me like ping-pong balls at a carnival game. I stared at the wall behind them. I nodded politely, focused entirely on not unraveling.

I heard the same geneticist who had met me with the chaplain less than two weeks earlier say that Lorelei would likely never walk, talk, or eat food by mouth. She told Michael and me that we both carry a rare recessive gene, meaning any future children would have a 25% chance of also having this disease. Then came the number: based on the two or three case studies available, Lorelei was the 31st documented case.

I blurted out, "There have only been thirty others at this hospital?"

The geneticist, realizing I wasn't fully processing what she was telling us, gently clarified: "Not at this hospital—on this planet."

And then, as if that wasn't enough, came the cherry on top: based on what little research existed, Lorelei was expected to live just two-to-five years.

She was the 31st documented case. Worldwide. And I was only supposed to have a couple of years with her.

How was I supposed to hold a lifetime of love and adventure, of bedtime stories, birthday celebrations, Girl Scout campouts, dreams, and future plans, when I was only given two to five years?

And then that word—*mitochondria*—lit up like a neon sign in my memory.

Of all the things for my brain to grab onto, it chose this memory. Suddenly I was back in tenth-grade biology, staring down at my glitter-covered styrofoam cell, the one I had spent hours perfecting. Every organelle labeled. The nucleus bedazzled. A mitochondrion outlined in puff-paint and tagged with washi tape.

That masterpiece of a cell lived in my childhood closet for over two decades because neither my mom nor I ever had the heart to throw it away.

And now that same word—*mitochondria*—was cracking my real heart wide open, in a far less sparkly way.

Mitochondria are the powerhouses of cells. That may be the only thing that public school kids remember from science class. But what does that actually mean?

Here's the quick version:

Your cells need energy to function. Mitochondria are where that energy is made. If your mitochondria are broken, your body does not get the fuel–the power–it needs. And without energy, things start to fall apart—slowly, then all at once.

Mitochondrial disease can affect every system in the body. Muscles, brain, heart, lungs, digestion, vision—everything. For Lorelei, and later Benji, this meant constant appointments, hospitalizations, scary conversations, and a lot of creative problem solving. Nothing was easy. Nothing was guaranteed.

Still foggy? Let me break it down for you in a more tangible way:

Take out your phone.

(Seriously. I know it's nearby.)

You know when your phone starts lying to you after a few years of owning it? After a full night of charging, it says the battery is at 100%, but by the time you've scrolled through a couple of reels and opened your email, it's already dropped to

27%? So you plug it in at 10 AM, carry backup chargers, and develop an unhealthy emotional attachment to battery-saving mode.

Now imagine your phone is a person. And that person wakes up every day with that kind of energy deficit. They just had a full night of sleep, so they should be at 100%. They're doing everything they can to keep running, but their systems are glitching. They can't hold a charge. They crash without warning. They need proper nutrition, rest, medication and care to keep going.

That was Lorelei. That is Benji.

My children's bodies don't produce energy properly. Their muscles are weak. Their development is delayed. Their stamina is unpredictable. Some days, their batteries die before we've even had breakfast. You can't see energy, but you can feel its absence. And when your child is running on empty, everything slows, everything storms, everything hurts.

Before I became a medical mom, I never thought about these things. I never wondered what life was like for a child who couldn't sit up on their own. I never thought about the courage it takes just to breathe or swallow or blink. And I never once considered what it must feel like to mother a child who might not outlive her goldfish. This diagnosis didn't just change Lorelei's life. It rewired mine.

Mitochondrial disease has taken so much from me, yes, but it also gave me a new perspective. That diagnosis, and my children's prognosis, forced me to see everything differently.

Lorelei lived with a failing battery and still lit up the world. She couldn't say "I love you," but she didn't have to. People felt it. Nurses, pharmacists, researchers, social workers, delivery drivers, strangers online—people who only met her through a glance or a giggle or a photo felt something sacred when they encountered her.

Because we were so isolated, I often worried that Lorelei did not have friends. That she was not able to make an impact on this world.

And when she died the messages poured in.

Cards from strangers. Emails from hospital staff. Notes from doctors, chaplains, CEOs, and even the therapy dog's handler. The security guard at the children's hospital sent a sympathy card. A research lab sent flowers. UPS drivers who had left boxes of medical supplies on our porch for years wrote messages about how they missed seeing her through the window.

They all told me the same thing: She mattered.

She wasn't just my girl.

She was everyone's girl.

This isn't a story about mitochondrial disease.

It is a story about a girl who lived on borrowed battery life and taught all of us what it means to truly *live like Lorelei.*

AUTHOR'S NOTE:

Science has come a long way since 2016, when we received the diagnosis that changed our lives. "Mitochondrial disease" is as general as saying "cancer." There are currently over 300 known mitochondrial diseases, with estimates suggesting there may be even more. FBXL4 mitochondrial disease had only been discovered in 2013, and the medical community did not begin to understand its function until a decade later, in 2023.

Today, children with FBXL4 Mito appear to fall on a broad spectrum of abilities, challenges, and outcomes. From the small but growing community we're building, it seems that many of these children are now living longer and more stable lives—when they receive the right medical and environmental support, and if they stay healthy.

Lovelei meeting Juliet, the first child diagnosed with FBXL4. Jules was an inspiration and beacon of hope for us.

Chapter 7

Seven

...the wholeness in the breaking.

There's something about the number seven. It has followed me, quietly, but consistently, through Lorelei's story. She was born seven weeks early. She spent 77 days in the NICU. She died on July seventh—which is 7/7. There are seven letters in her name. And now, somehow fittingly, this is Chapter Seven: the chapter where I first felt myself becoming whole. Not as a person, but as her mother. Not fixed. Not healed. But rooted. Fierce. Connected. Unshakably Lorelei's.

Lorelei was exactly nine weeks old (two weeks adjusted age) on the day she had her first surgery, to place her gastrostomy feeding tube, also known as a g-tube, a small device inserted through the abdomen to deliver nutrition directly to the stomach. She had finally reached the minimum weight to be cleared for surgery. Anesthesia is always risky, but for kids with mitochondrial disease, it can be catastrophic.

We knew she needed the surgery. My now-favorite

(though in that moment, very much not-so-favorite) neonatologist told me Lorelei would not be leaving his NICU without a g-tube. Spoiler: he was right. But I didn't want to believe him. I just wanted her home, and she couldn't consume enough calories without exhausting herself or aspirating.

It felt like I was giving up on her, even though I knew that this would be her ticket home. This surgery would get us closer to escaping the NICU hurricane and the grief, trauma, and heartache it carried in its wake.

We arrived early on the morning of her surgery. They made us sign paperwork with terrifying disclaimers. We kissed her goodbye and handed her off to the team who wheeled her away behind swinging doors, into the operating room. When it was over, they told us the surgery had gone well, and she was back in her NICU pod recovering.

It was the first time in nine weeks that I didn't stay at the hospital late into the night. She did not need to be bottle fed; she needed rest. And so did I.

It's wild how rest can feel like abandonment when you're a mother whose child lives on the edge of survival. I wanted to believe rest was a gift. But in that moment, it felt like betrayal.

The plan was to slowly begin introducing milk through her brand new g-tube the next day. For nine straight weeks, I had sat beside her isolette for as long as they would let me. I tried to feed her. I held her hand during tests. I hovered. I learned to decode the monitors. I memorized every beep and alarm. But that night was different. That night, I went home.

We had finally moved into our new house. (Author's note: 10/10 would not recommend building a house while pregnant and moving into said house during a NICU stay.) Furniture was sparse and boxes were still everywhere, but for the first time, we had family over. There was pizza. Laughter. And for a brief moment, despite the looming feeling that someone was missing, it felt like we were doing something normal.

As we got ready for bed, I looked at Michael and said, "I just feel like I should be there. I feel it."

He reminded me that I had been at the hospital every day for ten weeks, including my own weeklong preeclampsia stay before Lorelei was born.

"You need to rest," he said. "She's in good hands."

I wanted to believe him. Between commuting to and from the NICU, the hours spent at her bedside, pumping breast-milk around the clock, moving into our new home and still physically recovering from the emergency c-section, I was beyond exhausted.

So I conceded. I did not listen to that voice telling me I needed to be with her. I put the breast pump away and climbed into bed.

Five minutes later the phone rang.

"Mrs. Geoghegan? There has been an incident."

SOMEONE HURT MY BABY.

And I wasn't there.

It would take me years, and a lot of therapy, to realize just how much that night hardened me into the anxious, protective mother I am. That night is the reason I never, ever leave when my children are in the hospital. Not for a shower. Not for a meal. Not for "you need to rest" speeches. Because I wasn't there. And someone broke her.

Sometimes the most defining moments in motherhood aren't the ones where we were present, laughing, bonding, making memories. Sometimes the moments that change us most are the ones we weren't there for, and wish like hell we had been. The missed moments. The ones we replay. The ones we long to rewrite. They etch themselves into us—especially when the chance to be there again is gone.

The guilt lingers, but so does the love. And maybe, in some bittersweet way, that ache becomes part of the bond too.

Lorelei had been through her first surgery, a scary but successful g-tube placement. She was supposed to be resting and healing. Instead, during a routine IV placement, someone fractured her tiny femur. A spiral break. Her leg snapped.

Not gently. Not quietly. It wasn't a soft tissue injury or a minor twist. It was a spiral fracture: twisted and broken so violently that if I had carried her into the emergency room with that kind of injury, they would have called Child Protective Services. Spiral fractures don't happen easily. In medicine, these fractures often trigger abuse investigations because they suggest someone twisted the limb, not just bumped it. They require a forceful, wrenching motion, something no newborn should ever experience.

That's how bad it was.

But no one called. No one reported it. And we were left shattered.

It took a week and plenty of visits from the hospital's legal department before anyone would give us answers. It was confirmed that Lorelei did not have weak or brittle bones. The nurse who caused the injury claimed she heard a "pop," but assumed it was Lorelei's diaper. She didn't alert a doctor. She didn't ask for an X-ray. She just thought Lorelei was being fussy. And Lorelei—my nine-week-old, six-pound, post-op, medically fragile daughter—laid in her crib and cried for three hours. In pain. Alone. Unmedicated.

In NICUs, every beep is logged. Every diaper is tracked. But somehow, Lorelei's cries slipped through... while I was across town, lying in bed, trying to convince myself that rest made me a good mother.

It wasn't until the night-shift nurse arrived and did her routine assessment that anyone realized something was very wrong. Lorelei's pain was too much, even for a baby who had just had abdominal surgery. Her left leg wasn't moving. It was swelling.

Someone hurt my child.

She cried for hours.

I wasn't there.

♥♥♥♥♥♥♥

THE GUILT WAS UNBEARABLE. I had known. I had felt it. I had said it out loud and I didn't listen to my intuition.

Deep in my core, I know that I could not have changed the situation, whether I was at her bedside or at home. But that was the night that taught me to listen to my gut. That was the night I became her advocate, her protector.

There's a cost to that kind of learning. But there's also a gift.

That night taught me that Lorelei and I had a bond that was unbreakable, even if her femur wasn't.

This is when I started to understand what it meant to mother her, not just keep her alive. This was the beginning of truly being Lorelei's Mama. Not just a visitor to her bedside. Not just a cow hooked up to a breast pump.

I thought becoming a mother was supposed to happen at birth. But for some of us, it happens in the heartbreak—when something inside us stands up and says, "never again." This was the night I became her companion. Her protector. Her person.

She was mine. And I was hers.

Strangely, it was this broken night that made me feel whole. I didn't have all the pieces, and I never would. Motherhood isn't about having all the pieces. It's about knowing which pieces matter most and refusing to let go of them. The fracture didn't just mark Lorelei's femur; it marked the moment I stepped fully into my role as her mother. Fierce. Attuned. Unapologetic.

And maybe it's no coincidence that this is Chapter Seven.

Seven: the number of completion, spiritual fullness, inner knowing, and divine connection. Seven colors in a rainbow. Seven days in a week. Seven seas and seven continents. Seven wonders.

It is also the number that connects me to Lorelei.

She spent 77 days in the NICU. She died on 7/7.

Lorelei is magic. And our bond is sacred.

That night, I ignored the whisper in my gut and learned the hardest way. Magic doesn't usually shout. Sometimes, it's just a whisper inside your soul, quiet and steady in the darkest days, in the eye of the storm. But it's real. It's pure. It's love.

Chapter 8

What to Unexpect When Expecting

...and other things books never taught me about having a child.

We didn't carry her out of the NICU the way I thought we would. While I made sure she had a cute outfit, there was no sleepy newborn tucked into a classic car seat. Instead, Lorelei was strapped into something that looked like a glorified doll cradle. It was a car seat bed, the kind they give babies who can't sit upright because they have a broken femur. And her outfit of the day had to accommodate her tiny chicken leg wrapped in neon pink bandages.

She had spent the first months of her life fighting to survive, and now, what was supposed to be another celebratory milestone, her NICU graduation, became a scene where she was wheeled out of the hospital in a contraption that screamed "this really isn't normal." We left with support equipment, suction machines, feeding tube supplies, and an intimidating binder, thicker than my wedding planning folder, overflowing with discharge instructions.

This wasn't the story the baby books told. There was no

chapter titled, *"How to Secure a Feeding Pump to the Carseat Bed for Continuous Feeds While Driving Home."*

Baby books did not have milestone pages for the events we were about to face:

- ☑ First apnea alarm at home
- ☑ First time your baby vomited lifesaving medications all over your bed
- ☑ First time dog knocked over feeding pump pole and ripped the feeding tube out of your baby's belly
- ☑ First emergency call to the on-call hospice team

The drive home was quiet. Too quiet. I kept looking at Lorelei while Michael slowly drove through the Midtown Tunnel, thinking, *"hooray, they just let us take her home!"* but also *"oh crap, they just let us take her home!"* I wanted so badly to feel peace. To feel like this was a joyful moment. But I was scared. I was exhausted. I was grieving the loss of the version of motherhood I expected.

Just a few months prior, I had a vision of walking our baby into our brand-new home. I would look like a mom who had just had a blissful birthing experience. We would snap a picture of the family, with the border collie and golden retriever, in front of a tacky, six-foot-tall pink stork sign in the yard that announced the name and weight of our new arrival.

Instead, I came home to a house that looked more like a pediatric recovery ward than a nursery. Medical supplies lined the counters. Alarms echoed through the walls. I wasn't just a new mom. I was a nurse. A crisis manager. A full-time, unpaid specialist in the rarest condition I had never heard of until it hijacked our lives.

The first few weeks at home were foggy. This was survival mode in its purest form.

We lived in three-hour increments, ruled by medications, tube feeds, pumping schedules, and charting Lorelei's oxygen saturation like nurses chugging caffeine on night shift. My shirt was always stained. Lorelei's monitor cords were always tangled. My brain felt mushy, my boobs hurt, my hair was a mess, and everything was always spinning around me like someone had poured everything into a blender and forgotten to hit stop.

I didn't want visitors. Not because I didn't love people, but because I couldn't stand the questions. The tilted heads. The pity. The way people would glance at the machines and try to hide the fact that they were afraid to ask what any of them did.

I didn't know how to answer the polite, "How's the baby?" or even worse, "Is she feeling better?" I never knew if people wanted the truth or the shiny, happy, highlight reel. And I didn't have the energy to decipher which version they were ready for, or how much of the truth I needed to protect them from. Years into this journey, it still never feels fair to drop the full weight of our reality on someone just trying to make small talk in the Target checkout line. But it also doesn't feel fair that I have to smile and nod like I am not holding my breath every day.

While I may have the words now, back then I didn't know how to explain what it felt like to silence an alarm and wonder if it was a glitch or something that could take her from me. I didn't know how to describe the cold, clinical fear of relying on machines that had become part of our everyday existence or the mental gymnastics of trying to stay calm while scanning her face for signs of distress.

It wasn't just that she was medically fragile. It was that the hurdles we faced in the NICU had rewired me to be constantly aware of that fragility, while still the world expected me to carry on like a "normal" mom who walks around the neighborhood with an adorable baby in a cute stroller.

Nobody prepares you for this. Not the books. Not the birthing classes. Not the registry checklists, which never typically include "pulse oximeter" or "g-tube button pads."

Somewhere in the middle of that chaos, a whisper started to grow louder inside me: This cannot be all there is. This disease cannot win.

I didn't want to look back and realize that while we kept her alive, we forgot to let her live.

Lorelci's life was being measured in medication doses and symptom logs. I didn't want her story to be only hospital stays and survival records. But I didn't know how to "let her be little" when I was only trained how to keep her alive.

That's when I started the bucket list. Not the Morgan Freeman–Jack Nicholson kind, where grumpy old men go skydiving and eat caviar in the Alps. Ours involved sparkles, Girl Scout cookies, and princesses. It wasn't formal at first— more of a silent promise: if we were going to do this, really do this, then we were going to make it magical. We were going to work towards memories, not just milestones. We were going to chase joy with the same urgency we chased stable vitals.

We were going to say yes to glitter and costumes and pony parties in the backyard. Because even if I didn't know how long we had, I was damn well going to make sure that time was full.

There was no linear path forward, just a series of moments where we had to decide if joy was worth the risk.

Looking at life's challenges and adversities, and then forcing yourself to make an active decision to overcome them is far from easy. There were so many times when it really would have been easier to just live a basic, safe, uneventful life that the world believed was best for disabled children, and that science said she required.

Maybe I was selfish in wanting the memories for myself, but maybe part of it was for her too—even if she didn't fully understand and wouldn't live long enough to keep them. Either way, I made the decision that the difficulties of mitochondrial disease would not win.

Other than that one mom at the zoo who pulled me aside and scolded me for suctioning my child in the parking lot, most people asked, gently, hesitantly, why we didn't just stay home. Why did we try so hard when she probably didn't understand? Why risk the energy, the germs, the chaos for camping trips or Halloween costumes, when she couldn't trick-or-treat, let alone eat the candy?

They didn't say it to be cruel. But the question hung heavy: *Why go to so much trouble?*

Because joy was the only thing that made the rest of it bearable. And maybe, just maybe, it was the thing that kept us all alive.

It started slowly—vacations that looked a little different

than our friends'. Instead of hopping on planes or visiting busy theme parks, we went camping. Not the rustic, deep-woods kind. The glamping in a seafoam green vintage camper kind of camping. We had electricity. And walls. And a pulse oximeter charging on the side table next to marsh-mallows.

Camping gave us the freedom to travel without the fear of germs swarming us in crowded hotel lobbies or airplanes. We could control the environment, sanitize everything and stay close to nature while staying close to Lorelei's needs.

Lorelei had a way of always rewriting the script at the last minute. Our planned beach vacation? We spent the first half of the week with a surprise hydrocephalus diagnosis and an emergency shunt placement, then joined the family for the last few days.

A peaceful Mother's Day camping trip? Abruptly ended by one of the scariest out-of-hospital crashes of her life. Lorelei's body suddenly spiraled into what we later learned was her first autonomic crisis outside of the day she was born. Unfortunately, "autonomic storming," as the doctors called it, became more and more common throughout her life. Her nervous system would go haywire, flooding her body with adrenaline and sending her heart rate, blood pressure, and temperature skyrocketing. In the case of "The Mother's Day Crash of 2017," it forced us to pack up the campsite, drive home at midnight, and race to the ER. Over time, we learned how to better support her through these storms.

But despite one plot twist after another, we still kept trying. We made the decision over and over to create joy in the midst of the storm, because we promised her a life worth living, not just surviving. Even when it was hard. Even when it felt unfair. Even when it would've been easier to shut down and stay home and stop hoping altogether.

Regardless of her disease, her age, her lack of verbal communication skills, Lorelei was calling all the shots. She made it abundantly clear. She would accept my plans and then execute them using her own creative liberties. Whether it was our vacations or her doctor appointments, she was in charge. Not the diagnosis. Not the specialists. Not even the cast members at the entrance of Magic Kingdom. We followed her lead, and she taught everyone around her how to keep living.

I used to cry after the parties. Not during. Eh, sometimes during, amidst the glitter and singing, as I helped her blow out candles on the cake she could only lick but not eat.

And then later, when it was quiet, I'd sit in the laundry room, holding a sparkly tutu crusted with puke, and wonder: *Was that too much? Did I push her too hard? Did I push myself too hard? Did I choose wrong?* Because while she fell asleep smiling, I stayed awake unraveling.

Choosing joy meant choosing to live in the tension: the fear of what it might cost her, and the ache of what it cost me.

I USED to plan my life in ink. Sharp lines. Bold appointments. Color-coded, well-labeled tabs.

But somewhere in those early years, I found myself staring at a planner that no longer made sense. Plans kept getting erased, literally. Canceled. Rescheduled. Postponed for feeding tube site infections, medication reactions, and plot twists with names like autonomic storm and metabolic acidosis.

Planning used to be the one thing that kept me sane and safe and organized. But now there were days I wanted to toss the whole damn calendar in the trash. What was the point? I struggled with the loss of control, but more than that, the lack of ability in fixing this for my daughter.

Planning began to look different. Because even though plans changed, there were still appointments to track. Specialists to remember. Medication doses to log. Life might've become unpredictable, but it was still packed.

Eventually, I gave in and bought erasable pens. It felt like a concession at first, like I was surrendering to a life without permanence, without real planning. But in time, it felt like power. Like flexibility. Like choosing hope over rigidity. Looking for joy within the grief.

Joy didn't mean I wasn't grieving. It meant I was fighting back with cupcakes and costume changes. With backyard pony parties and painted toenails and Girl Scout cookies by the caseload. Every joyful thing we did was a middle finger to the medical case studies that never promised us tomorrow.

♥♥♥♥♥♥♥

THERE WERE plenty of things she never checked off her bucket list, by the way. But, together we accomplished a lot:

- ☑ Catch a baseball at a Norfolk Tides game.
- ☑ Meet the JMU Duke Dog.
- ☑ Go to Disney World.
- ☑ Stand, actually weight bear, with Mickey Mouse.
- ☑ Show Anna and Elsa that Lorelei is a real princess like them.
- ☑ Take boat rides with Grandma and Papa B.
- ☑ Take a ballet class (with Miss Meredith).
- ☑ Get a goldendoodle companion pup.
- ☑ Have Dada walk her down the aisle as the flower girl for Auntie and Uncle Mister's wedding.
- ☑ Have a backyard pony party.
- ☑ Become a Girl Scout (and then sell 775 boxes of cookies to be later donated to doctors, nurses, and staff at the children's hospital).
- ☑ Go to Girl Scout camp with the proceeds from her cookie sales.

Lorelei and I couldn't write our family's future in permanent ink, so we doodled in glitter pens and neon hope instead.

Forever was never mine to offer her. Instead, I promised her everything else: sparkle, joy, chaos, and love.

And you better believe I kept my word.

♥♥♥♥♥♥♥

Chapter 9

Faith and Toothpaste

...and other lessons for Lorelei's foster mom.

"I don't know how you do it."

"How do you stay so positive with everything going on?"

I've always been open about my experiences as a medical mama, but people tell me what sets me apart isn't that I share my story—it's how I tell the whole thing: the alarms and the belly laughs, the bathroom sobs and the small wins that kept us upright, the struggles and the hope.

That same honesty eventually led me to podcasting. In 2019, I connected with Diane, a fellow mito mom I'd never met in person but whose life felt uncannily similar to mine. We both knew we couldn't be the only ones carrying these feelings, despite the isolation we'd each felt. Armed with dark humor and sarcasm, we started recording our conversations, and from that the *When Autumn Comes Podcast* was born.

A disability advocacy filmmaker, and fellow rare disease parent, once told me he liked that I don't use a fake podcasting voice on my show—that I sound like myself, not overly professional or polished, that I'm politely unfiltered. I'm pretty sure what he actually said was that I wasn't 'super sweet like other podcasting moms,' but I chose to take it as a compliment.

Many of us have our own version of that "polished voice," the one we use when we want the world to believe we're okay. Our talk track. Our elevator intro. The script we stick to until someone earns the right to hear the unscripted version. But it's the people we meet in those rare, unpolished conversations—the ones over coffee when another mom whispers the thing she thought only she was feeling, or in the OR waiting room where two strangers hug through tears as they finally admit how scared they really are. It's in those moments—when we are brave enough to let someone in—that hope feels possible and connection feels real.

And yet, not everyone knew how to meet me in that unpolished space. When Lorelei was a baby, I noticed people fell into categories. A rare few just sat with me in the storm, their quiet presence saying more than any words could. Others offered religious books and platitudes, like BOGO life rafts I hadn't asked for—sometimes well-meaning, sometimes suffocating. And then there were the blunt ones who, right in the middle of my darkest days, asked, "How do you believe in God—or in anything good—when this is what you're facing?" Maybe those questions had merit somewhere down the road, but not when I was gasping for air. On those days, it just felt rude.

Most people didn't fit neatly into one category. Some handed me a book *and* showed up with dinner. Some asked questions I wasn't ready for but still stood beside me when I couldn't answer. Some tried, awkwardly but earnestly, to stitch hope into conversations where words would never be enough.

Crises reveal people's default settings: some sit in silence, some offer fixes, some voice the hardest questions. None of it was perfect. None of it was entirely wrong. But each response showed me something about who they were—and who I was—during the storm.

My best friends fell into category number one. The twos and threes weren't strangers. They were friends, family, and acquaintances who simply couldn't reconcile the collision of innocence and suffering they saw in front of them. Some were deeply faithful, devout Christians, observant Jewish friends, asking not from judgment, but from disbelief that faith could coexist with what they were witnessing. I could see many of them quietly wrestling with their own version of our Creator, trying to reconcile how a loving, kind God could allow innocent, beautiful children to be born with genetic errors and downright shitty mitochondria.

As faithful, optimistic, overachieving humans, most of us are raised to believe there's a certain moral math to life: if you're good, work hard, believe the right things, and pray enough, then you'll be spared the worst. We like to think hard things follow a pattern—that storms come with warning, that lightning only strikes in certain places. That our plane will not crash. That our babies will be healthy. This moral math is comforting, but it's also an illusion.

We tell ourselves we'll be safe if we pray harder, eat cleaner, and think more positively. We whisper tiny prayers and make private bargains at the first sign of dark skies, promising to be better if the clouds just pass us by. But pain isn't that tidy, and storms don't check your résumé before they hit. They just arrive—sometimes with warning, often without—and they don't care if you've done everything "right."

When the water rises, it seeps into the places we thought were untouchable, finding the cracks in our carefully built foundations. And maybe that's why we're so quick to build levees around other people's grief—by changing the subject, offering platitudes, or holding them at arm's length. We're not doing it to protect them. We're doing it to keep their pain from seeping into our own lives, or worse, into our own faith.

Because if we let the dark, painful, grief-filled water in, we might have to wrestle with the same questions in which they're drowning. We might have to face the possibility that our Creator isn't who we thought He was, that the moral math doesn't exist, or that faith isn't the safety net we believed it to be.

I RARELY FEEL ANGRY. It's simply not my default setting. I know many parents in my situation who wrestle with deep, justified rage: at the diagnosis, at the trauma that caused it, at the fact that their child died. Anger is valid, and it deserves space. But for me, accepting—maybe not wanting to accept, but still accepting—that this was the life I'd be living alongside my children and my husband allowed me to trust God more, not less. It kept me hope-filled and present for both of my kids.

And while I am far from perfect, learning to accept the plot twists I'm handed has helped me loosen my white-knuckle grip on control, reminding me there's a higher power steering this ship, and I'm just along for the ride.

Part of accepting Lorelei's disease, and the absurdity that my child would die before me, was this:

I saw myself as a foster parent for God.

My job was to keep these kids for as long as I was supposed to keep them. To love them as hard as humanly possible. To give them the fullest, richest lives I could, and to learn with them—and later, to learn because of them.

I believed that when the time came, it would be my sacred job to walk Lorelei, hand-in-hand, as far as I could to the gate of Heaven... and to trust that God would meet us there.

I believed that with my whole heart, but faith—like trust—only proves its strength when it's tested. And mine wasn't a single, cinematic showdown. It was more like the SATs in high school: long, exhausting, and broken into endless sections obviously written by a committee of joyless trolls.

My test came in the form of countless small fires to put out: white-hot, "someone's-going-to-hear-about-this" moments with insurance companies, lab results, hospital billing departments. But sometimes, it was worse than paper-work and phone calls. A nurse broke my daughter's femur. There was no apology, no consequence, no justice. We were left to carry both the break and the silence around it.

I've been furious at the systems, at the red tape, at the

sheer incompetence that sometimes stood between my child and the care she needed—the care she deserved. But that fury was never aimed at God, the universe, or my children. I believe God loves them even more than I do, and I know the failures belong to broken systems, not to Him. And my anger was never turned towards Lorelei and Benji, because they were the ones carrying the weight—I was the one called to carry them.

Still, faith doesn't only get tested in the headline-worthy battles. Sometimes the most jarring moments sneak in on quiet, ordinary mornings. The kind where you're standing in your bathroom, toothbrush in hand, thinking about your grocery list, and then suddenly you're face-to-face with the kind of anger that makes your knees go weak. The kind of moment you don't just remember, you feel in your bones years later.

The thing about big feelings is they don't knock first. They're impolite houseguests who don't wait for an invitation. They show up whenever they want and trash the place to make sure you don't forget they were there. They crash through the door of your everyday life, whether you're in the middle of a meeting, driving to the grocery store, or brushing your teeth on a quiet morning.

One morning, those feelings didn't just knock—they kicked the bathroom door off its hinges. The world stayed perfectly ordinary, but inside, something shifted so completely I knew I wouldn't walk away the same. If I had to point to a single time God grabbed me by the shoulders and said, "Listen up!," this was it.

Lorelei had recently come home from the NICU, and I

was standing in our bathroom, finally alone for a few minutes. Halfway lost in thought while brushing my teeth, I was t-boned by a wave of fury. It came out of nowhere, so fast and so sharp that I nearly spat toothpaste onto the brand-new, sparkly clean mirror. One second I was going through a normal, forgettable morning routine; the next, I was internally shouting at God with a rage I'd never felt before.

Part of that anger was because of the pain my daughter was in, but mostly it was the crushing unfairness of it all. It wasn't fair that everyone else seemed to be getting the life I thought I deserved, the one I had worked for, the one I believed I'd been promised. The story I thought belonged to me was torn away mid-chapter, and I was left with a plot I never agreed to read, let alone live. I saw every milestone I thought I'd lost: slumber parties, prom dresses, and normal-parent anxieties of watching Lorelei behind the wheel of a car for the first time rather than regularly being wheeled into an operating room.

Somewhere in that fury, I thought of her sleeping in the next room—so tiny, so new, so terrifyingly rare—and wondered if she'd ever know a life without storms. I didn't have the words for it yet, but part of me already sensed she would end up teaching me more about faith, trust, and living than I could ever teach her. Back then, my version of trust looked a lot different. I was only months removed from the version of me who stood in the CoverGirl aisle at Target, confidently believing, "God wouldn't give me a sick child." That kind of trust felt unshakable, built on the assumption that faith was a guarantee against pain, not something that would carry me through it. I was treating faith like an insurance policy, not realizing it was actually my life raft.

And now here I was, standing in my picture-perfect new home, living a reality I couldn't have imagined even in my worst nightmares. A reality where my daughter's life hinged on medical equipment and medications to stay alive. A reality measured in grams gained, oxygen levels, and follow-up hospital visits.

It wasn't because I had done something to "deserve" this path, or because I hadn't prayed hard enough, or because I was strong enough to handle it. And for the love of all things, it wasn't because God only gives special people special needs children. (Author's note: never, ever say this to anyone. It's not comforting and it's not biblical. It is hurtful.)

But this was my reality now. I was a caregiver to a rare baby, knowing there was a 25% chance that any of our future babies would have the same cruel disease. I was dropped straight into the thick of this storm, one I didn't know was brewing. Sometimes the plot twists make no sense, not from the middle of the story, anyway. It's only in hindsight that we can see the unique, crooked, bumpy path we were actually on.

And there I was, toothpaste splattering into the sink, staring into the mirror, trying to understand, just like I'd seen so many people around me do, trying to reconcile the God I thought I knew with the God who had allowed this to happen.

And then, just as quickly, I felt the voice say: It's okay to be angry with me. It's okay to say it and feel it. It's okay to believe none of this is fair. But then you must choose: will this be the anchor that drowns you or the light that helps you navigate through the storm?

It wasn't judgment. It was an invitation to move anger somewhere else instead of letting it calcify inside me.

Every one of us will face a moment like that—maybe not with God, maybe not with grief, probably not because of a rare disease—but a moment where we have to decide: will this break me down or break me open?

Something will pop up out of nowhere and your plans will fall apart. It could be as small as a coffee date that gets canceled or as life-altering as a marriage ending. A missed flight or losing a job you loved. Whatever it is, the ground shifts. And in that split second, you have to ask yourself: *How will I handle this change? Will it be the anchor that drags me under, or the wind that carries me somewhere new?*

In that moment, I knew: if I wanted to truly learn whatever lessons I was supposed to learn during my time on Earth, if I wanted Lorelei's life—and by extension, my own life—to matter as much as possible beyond her disease, anger could not be my anchor.

The validation of that voice, and the confirmation that it is okay to feel upset about my circumstances, brought an unexpected peace. The moment passed, and that particular kind of anger never returned. Instead, with excessively clean teeth, I started looking for what Lorelei seemed to see without effort: that trust isn't a thing you feel once and keep forever, it's a choice you make over and over, even when you're still standing in the storm.

IT WAS normal for us to never be more than three feet away from a suction machine—whether at home, in the hospital, or on the road. Lorelei spent most of her life uncomfortably battling excessive mucus. At one point, I even gave a presentation to the new residents at the children's hospital and told them—half joking, but also absolutely serious—that if anyone could figure out a way to give Lorelei some respite from her mucus, I'd hand them a week's vacation in a oceanfront house. No one ever did.

Her lack of muscle tone meant the mucus would either form a plug in her throat or cause her to vomit several times a day. It was terrifying, uncomfortable, messy, and downright dangerous. I often had to hold her down and deep suction her with a long catheter to clear the secretions from her throat. It was horrendous—but it was necessary. She hated the feeling. So did I. But we both knew it was what her body needed, and she unconditionally trusted me to help her through it.

Lorelei was the one who taught me what trust looked like. She didn't just trust—she TRUSTED. She trusted God and the universe, strangers in the hospital, and her Mama and Dada when things were bad. Trust wasn't an abstract idea—it was lived in suction tubes, hospital rooms, and the messiest, scariest moments of her life. And somewhere along the way, I took a page from her playbook and began to trust right alongside my girl. If she could do it, so could I.

That bathroom revelation, the one that taught me the difference between being mad at broken mitochondria and being mad at God, is what allowed me to keep hope intact. It freed me to trust that even if I couldn't fix everything, something bigger than myself was working alongside me. And in that trust, I could stay steady for Lorelei and, later, for Benji.

When things got hard, Lorelei looked up. Scratch that. Lorelei *always* looked up. Not only because she was physically unable to sit up so she laid on the floor, staring at the ceiling of our living room like it was her job, but because there was always a higher plan in action for her. One that was so much bigger than me, and definitely bigger than Lorelei's monumental hair. From day one, we all felt it in our core: she was here for a reason, a mission, a purpose, a lesson. One that only she and God seemed to understand.

Like most humans in our anxious, non-trusting society, it takes a lot for me to fully trust anyone. But in medical parenthood, you don't get the luxury of building trust slowly. You meet doctors for the first time as they examine your baby in the ER. You don't have time to check their credentials. You just have to hand over your child—and your heart—and hope you've placed them in capable hands.

At some point, after watching Lorelei exhibit more unwavering grace and trust than most adults are capable of, I was yet again reminded that a lot was out of my control, while *everything* was out of Lorelei's control. I had two options: fight it all, rowing upstream in a barely floating pirate ship, or surrender to the wind and current while doing my part to keep the ship afloat, and my crew safe. I'm still learning the practice of surrendering and trusting, but Lorelei gave me the map and became my compass.

Turns out, surrender isn't giving up, it's just trading the

illusion of control for the reality of peace. Maybe that's the whole thing about faith: it's not about pretending storms won't come, or believing the ending will always be what you hoped for. It's about trusting that when the sky finally clears, you'll be able to look up and see something worth holding onto.

Trusting that the universe has your back, and that your God has not betrayed or abandoned you isn't something you do once. Faith is more like brushing your teeth: daily, often boring, incredibly repetitive, and good for you. That morning in the bathroom, foamy-mouthed and furious, I didn't realize I was starting a habit. Not just good dental hygiene. I was creating a habit of showing up for trust, even when it was messy, even when the storm was raging right outside the window.

Chapter 10

Finding Her Voice

...one eye gaze and one side-eye at a time.

When we received the diagnosis and were told that most children with FBXL4 mitochondrial disease could not talk, I was speechless. The idea of having a child who was unable to speak absolutely terrified me, because being understood isn't a luxury, it's a human need—with or without words.

Logistically, how would I know what she needed? Would I ever hear Lorelei say, *"I love you, Mama"*? Would I know how to care for her (and later Benji) if she couldn't tell me what hurt? Could we have a real relationship if we never had a conversation?

I repeatedly asked doctors and therapists if there were signs or symptoms that could tell us whether Lorelei would ever speak. I begged the neurologist to take a closer look at Lorelei's MRI, to tell us what her brain damage could mean for her future. She gently replied, *"Mom, the MRI isn't a crystal ball."*

I hated that answer. I wanted facts. I wanted proof. I needed science to be wrong. I felt it in my soul, but I wanted to hear my daughter tell me that I was her best friend.

Despite my reservations, I clumsily made it work. Friends would ask, "How do you know what she needs?" And honestly? I didn't know. I just *knew*.

I knew Lorelei better than anyone on the entire planet. I knew her sounds, her cues, the subtle shifts in her eyes. I knew her vomit triggers, her storming signs, her joy, her sass, her fear. Her voice may not have sounded like yours, but it was there, loud, clear, and uniquely hers.

While she and I communicated on a soul-level, Lorelei communicated with everyone in different ways. She was like a little blond-haired Yoda. She was an old soul, so if you paused for a moment, gave her a second, and really took it in, she would share more wisdom with you through her eyes than typical five-year-olds do with their mouths. You just had to give her time and creative liberties to get her point across.

Lorelei had what we lovingly called *The Resting Mito Face,* and just like its cousin *RBF*, it spoke volumes. She would clap for yes or no questions. She would look toward what she wanted. She couldn't point, but she had a pretty fierce naughty finger. If you gave her time and space, she would use nonverbal communication to tell you everything you needed to know.

And then Ms. Cat entered our lives.

Ms. Cat, her speech language pathologist, was passionate, persistent, and patient. Despite the degree in a fancy frame on my wall that says I am an expert in Communication Studies, it was Ms. Cat who continued to remind me that not all communication is traditional. She never put Lorelei in a box, even when I let medical trauma whisper limits into my ear.

Doctors and science had said Lorelei would probably never talk. They didn't say she wouldn't communicate.

Ms. Cat was the one who first introduced us to augmentative communication devices. Until then, my only frame of reference was Stephen Hawking on *The Big Bang Theory*. I was that clueless. But Lorelei wasn't. With a Tobii Dynavox computer and her gaze, she told the world what she wanted.

At first, it was simple things. With a couple pictures, she could answer yes or no questions better than a Magic 8 Ball. As Lorelei's disease progressed and her body became more tired, she learned to use her eyes to "press" buttons on the screen. When she was feeling social—because let's be real, sometimes none of us feel like talking—she relied less on reaching for things and more on her Tobii Talker to express herself.

Her personality and sense of humor came through quickly. In speech therapy, Ms. Cat would set up an activity and Lorelei would immediately say, "I want. All done." Ms. Cat kept her game face on, but I could feel pride radiating from her because Lorelei was making choices, speaking her mind.

At the hospital, Lorelei was curled up with me in bed, watching movies on her iPad after a long day, when Chaplain Anne walked in to check on us. Before Anne even finished sanitizing her hands and stepping fully into the room, Lorelei glanced at her screen and declared, "I want. All done. Goodbye. All done. Goodbye. All done. Goodbye." The chaplain laughed, I buried my face in my hands, and together we realized: this little girl had opinions. In the middle of our PICU exhaustion, we were so proud of her for finding her voice, advocating for herself, and using the computer she had to do it.

One morning, while I was preparing her food for the day and dancing like a fool in our kitchen, Lorelei got my attention and then used her Tobii Talker to say, "I love you."

I dropped to my knees, cupped her face, and stared into her eyes. "I love you too, Doodle. Mama loves you too," I whispered, laughing and crying all at once.

The moment shimmered, glitter and confetti scattering through the kitchen in my memory. They said she'd probably never talk. But that morning, Lorelei found her voice. Her sassy, loving, nontraditional voice—a voice that was greater and more beautiful than any expectation I'd ever had.

And as she discovered her voice, so did I.

I was slowly finding my voice as a caregiving mama, trusting my mom gut in the medical setting and stepping into what it meant to be her advocate. As we navigated this journey together, I found the courage to speak up about what was truly best for my daughter.

Simultaneously I was finding my voice as a mother, not just a caregiver. I was learning what my version of motherhood looked like, how I wanted to respond and react, what acts of love would shape the kind of mom—and the kind of woman—I was becoming.

Often I felt caught between roles: caregiver and mom. The one who keeps the child alive, and the one who simply wants to hold her. That tug-of-war lives in every parent: the instinct to protect and the ache to simply love.

That dichotomy, the tension between clinical logic and maternal instinct, came crashing down during one of the scariest moments of our journey: when I realized that loving her meant being willing to let her go... but also brave enough to let her stay.

IT WAS EARLY in our adventure, and I was still earning my stripes as a rare-disease medical mom. I found myself surrounded by medical equipment on the floor of a hotel bathroom in Orlando, Florida—googling "nearest children's hospital" and mapping the fastest route while Lorelei gasped for air beside me.

We were twelve hours from home. Lorelei was just shy of her second birthday, and I had brought her along with me to a work conference in the Sunshine State. Lorelei would stay in the hotel with Grandma and her nurse while I worked. The plan was simple: a few days of meetings followed by a few days of magic. Disney World was waiting, with princesses to wave at and Mickey Mouse to meet, both important items on that bucket list I was quietly building in my heart.

But on the last day of the conference, something wasn't right.

Lorelei wasn't acting like herself. She was withdrawn. She was weak. Her breathing changed, her color shifted, and my internal alarms were blaring. I tried all the tricks I had learned in our short medical life, but this time, we were facing the crossroads of hope and fear. It was time to go.

We rushed to the children's hospital, where triage took

one look at her and skipped us ahead. No forms. No waiting room fish tank. Just a fast pass of chaos because my kid was gasping for air.

After the viral panel, the ultimate F-bomb was delivered from a bewildered resident: Lorelei had the influenza B. The flu.

For a typical toddler, the flu meant fevers and Popsicles. For my child with mitochondrial disease, it was a potential death sentence.

At 11PM, the PICU attending came down to the ER. He was calm, steady and friendly. With his hands folded together in his lap, he sat across from me on the backless stool on wheels and gently said, "So... tell me about Lorelei."

I launched into her medical history without skipping a beat. I listed diagnoses, medications, vascular access needs, and the labs that needed to be run. I was halfway through telling him everything I thought he needed to know to keep her alive when he stopped me.

"No," he interrupted gently. "Tell me about Lorelei."

I sat there blankly. Perplexed and embarrassed at the same exact time.

He repeated himself. "Tell me about Lorelei. What does she like? Who is she?"

No one had ever asked me that before.

Not in that way. Not with that kind of humanity.

He wasn't asking about her lab values. He wanted to know who he was fighting for. He wanted to know what made her happy and what made her laugh.

I remember gripping the edges of my binder, trying to remember how to speak outside the language of diagnoses and previous discharge summaries. I fumbled out, "She loves music... her favorite colors are pink and aqua... she has a really funny sense of humor... and she loves *Frozen* and *Trolls*."

It felt like the first time someone had seen her not as a patient, but as a child.

It felt like the first time I was reminded I was a mom, and not just a caregiver.

❤❤❤❤❤❤

DAYS INTO THAT VACATION—I mean, hospital stay—hours after Micheal's last minute flight brought him to Orlando, Lorelei crashed. She had been holding her own against the flu, but as her body funneled precious energy toward fighting the virus, other vital systems began to fail.

I had run down the hall to take a quick, and very mediocre, shower, trying to squeeze in a sliver of normalcy. But when I stepped out, I heard the unmistakable blare of a crash code. Doctors, nurses, respiratory therapists—even a chaplain—were running.

They were running toward our room.

They were running toward my child.

And just like that, my body remembered. The last time, I wasn't there—*really* wasn't there—someone broke her femur. This time, I had left for five minutes. Five minutes of self-care. A quick shower. And in those five minutes, her body gave out. She crashed. And I wasn't there.

Lorelei's body was too weak to keep going without life support.

Cuddled in bed with her, tears streaming down my face, the intensivist looked me straight in the eyes and said, "What do you want to do, Mom? We can try. Or we can give her comfort with pain medicine, and you can hold her in her final moments. But you don't have long to decide."

And here's the part I don't usually say out loud: I was ready to let her go.

She was tired. I was tired. I didn't want her to suffer anymore. I was ready to wrap her in my arms and cuddle her to heaven.

There's a story in the Bible where two women come before King Solomon, both claiming to be the mother of the same child. To uncover the truth, Solomon says he'll cut the baby in half and give each woman a piece. One woman says, "Fine, divide him." But the other, the real mother, begs the king to give the baby to the other woman instead. She'd rather let him go than see him hurt.

That story echoed in my heart long before I understood why. Because that day, in that sterile, crowded PICU room, twelve hours from home, I knew what it meant to love someone so much you'd give them up to spare them pain. I was the mother begging to stop any form of pain my baby was going through. Not because I didn't want Lorelei. But because I loved her more than I loved the idea of keeping her.

And yet, I was also her caregiver. Her medical decision-maker. The one responsible for fighting for every ounce of life. I was standing in the space between two truths: The mother in me whispered, *let her rest.* The caregiver in me asked, *what else can we do?*

That's where so much of life is lived, in the middle of

contradiction, where clarity isn't clean, but love still leads. Motherhood is a brutal kind of love that teaches you to loosen your grip when everything in you wants to hold tighter.

But in the middle of that tension, Michael, my steady, hopeful, gut-check of a husband, spoke. Not as the "other woman" in Solomon's story, but as someone who loved Lorelei just as fiercely. "We have to give her the chance," he said. "How will we know what she's capable of if we don't offer her every ounce of support?"

So we did.

LORELEI WAS INTUBATED in Orlando for eight days, the longest they'd give us before letting her body prove whether it could come off the ventilator or not. Her vitals were a mess, swinging between terrifying and nonsensical. As I watched her struggle, I saw the same pattern I remembered from the day she was born. The same battle. The same signs. It felt like confirmation of something I'd always known deep down: she really had been dying the day she arrived.

There were moments during that month-long "vacation" when things got dark. Really dark. Even the attending noticed how suffocating it had become. For days she had been telling me to leave, and for days I had refused. When she stopped by Lorelei's room one afternoon—off the clock, heels still on—she found me camped out by the bedside again. Lorelei was asleep, Michael was there, and I had no excuse. She looked at me and simply said, "We're going for a walk."

I thought she meant around the hospital. Fine. I could do

that. Florida in January felt almost like mercy compared to our brick-wall view from our PICU room window. But then she kept walking—past the hospital doors, into the parking garage. Weird, but okay. Then she opened the car door and said, "Get in." Who was I to argue with the doctor who had just intubated my daughter? So I got in. I texted Michael: *the doctor just kidnapped me—in her car! I think I'm okay...?*

She drove us to a quiet neighborhood and pulled over by a lake. In a blunt voice I assume is standard issue for all kidnappings, she said, "Get out." She began to swap her heels for sneakers and said, "When things get tough, I find a lake to walk around. Let's go." So we walked. She wasn't trying to fix anything or offer advice. She was simply walking beside me in the storm of that hospital stay.

Somewhere along that loop, our conversation drifted to logistics—the kind you should never have to think about while your child is intubated. I told her I'd been looking into how we'd get Lorelei's body home if she didn't make it. Turns out, both UPS and FedEx can transport human remains across state lines. Instead of shutting me down, she leaned right in, and I realized she was a safe person to share my dark humor that few can handle. She met me step-for-step, line-for-line, and we debated which shipping company would be best. It came down to branding. She smirked and offered, "If I was going to ship my daughter home, I would pick the one with a pop of purple." And I agreed, because UPS just screamed "cardboard sadness" to me.

It was the first time in a long time that I felt free to use my voice—my real voice. Not the polite caregiver voice, not the brave mom voice, but the sarcastic, irreverent, dark-humor voice that kept me alive in the shadows of all this. And instead of recoiling, she met me there. She showed me it was okay to let that voice out.

That walk, that lake, that conversation—that kidnapping —it was the respite I needed. It was humanity, love, and support in its purest, albeit nontraditional, form. And it ended up being the only fresh air I got until my support system from home flew into town.

My dad and sister rush to Florida, along with my closest friends, Caitlin and Jess. They came to sit in the uncertainty with us, to hold vigil while we waited to see what Lorelei would do. Watching them walk into that Florida hospital was heartbreaking, but also incredibly comforting, supportive, and surreal—that they would travel across states just to sit in the maybe with us.

But Lorelei lived. She proved all of us wrong. Again.

She lived three and a half more years.

Three and a half more years of sass and sparkle, of hospitalizations and homecomings. Three and a half more years of milestones no MRI could predict. Three and a half more years that included a "Disney Redo Trip" when everyone else thought I was insane. Three and a half more years of communicating in ways we never expected. Three and a half more years that also included becoming a big sister.

She lived long enough to say many, many more times, with her eyes, her stubbornness, and her Tobii Talker, "I'm not done yet."

And I wasn't either. Because it wasn't just Lorelei who found her voice in those years.

I figured out how to balance the voice of motherhood

with the voice of caregiving. I learned that both could exist, one fierce, one soft; one clinical, one intuitive. Sometimes they clashed. Sometimes they braided together. Sometimes one would take the lead while the other whispered and supported from the background. But they always led me back to her.

I found my voice. Not just the one that asked for second opinions or called out bad care, but the voice that reminded me I was still her mother, even when the hospital made me feel like an employee in my own story.

Through respiratory treatments and victory laps, sleepless nights and sparkly crowns, I was figuring out how to be both her nurse and her mama.

I started speaking up. I started trusting my gut. I started telling the truth, even when it was uncomfortable.

Lorelei taught me that you don't have to say a word to be loud. She didn't need a voice to make an impact. And neither did I. It turns out, silence doesn't mean absence. It just means you have to listen differently.

All done. Goodbye.
All done. Goodbye.
I love you. Goodbye.

♥♥♥♥♥♥♥

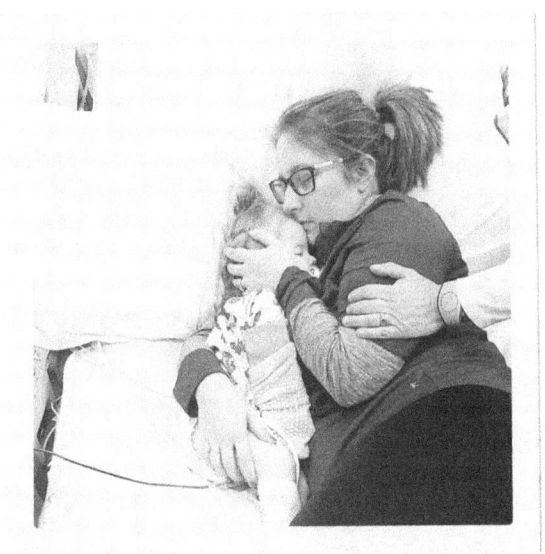

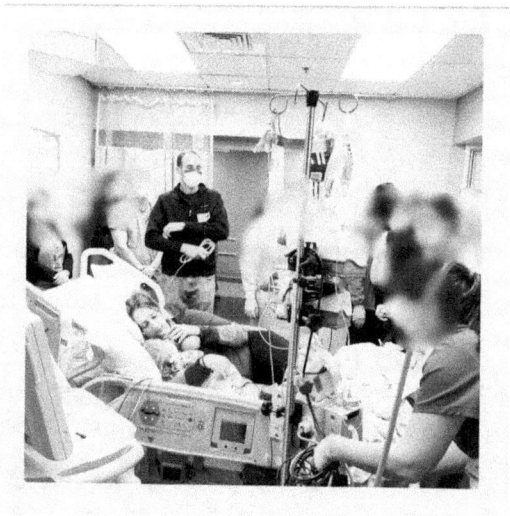

Chapter 11

Big Sister Era

...siblings, soulmates, and center stage.

L orelei was thriving in a way we hadn't seen before. The Florida crash, while terrifying, led us to add another doctor to our list of specialists—a palliative doctor who finally looked at the big picture. At first, the idea of adding a palliative doctor sounded abhorrent and unnecessary, but we had just witnessed the power of mitochondrial disease and knew we would need the support.

I quickly recognized her as a familiar face; she had been a resident when Lorelei was in the NICU. After finishing her residency, she returned to launch the first pain and palliative program at our children's hospital. She wasn't afraid of hard conversations. She became one of the first doctors to help us think about Lorelei beyond the daily crises—and, years later, she would be the one sitting beside us when Lorelei died.

I remember our first conversation with her after Florida. She asked why we were trying so hard to wean Lorelei off the pain meds prescribed there if she was finally thriving on them. Gently, she explained that a child like Lorelei would always need medications—and that her role was to help Lorelei live with the best quality of life possible, while giving us, her family, the best chance to make memories with her. It was hard to hear a medical professional say this out loud, but it also validated my deepest desire: to give Lorelei a full life, complete with her bucket list. She adjusted Lorelei's meds, eased her discomfort, and began supporting us as a family in ways we didn't even know we needed.

When a mom first hears the word *palliative,* the assumption is that it means end of life. But in the pediatric world, palliative often walks hand in hand with pain management. It doesn't mean giving up—it means choosing comfort, presence, and quality.

FOR THE FIRST time in a long time, we weren't just barely surviving. We were breathing. Resting. *Wondering.*

We'd faced the mito monster head-on in Orlando and somehow walked away stronger. Our confidence was shaky, but real. We knew what this disease could do, and we knew we could handle it. We knew Lorelei could handle it.

And with that space, a new question emerged: *Is someone missing?*

Michael and I danced around it for a while. The idea of another child felt equal parts reckless and redemptive. It wasn't about *trying again* for a second shot at typical parenthood. It was about that tiny, unshakable feeling that our family wasn't finished. Someone was missing. And I recognized that voice, the same intuition that told me I was pregnant with Lorelei before a test could confirm it. That voice was speaking again.

But we couldn't pretend it was a normal decision. Because the odds weren't normal. Our family was not normal.

Michael and I are only recessive carriers of the same faulty FBXL4 gene. Which meant there was a 25% chance of having another child with the same rare mitochondrial disease as Lorelei. We knew exactly what that meant now. We'd lived it.

We couldn't consider having another child unless we were ready to have *two* disabled children. Two children with mito. Two hospital rooms. Two wheelchairs. Two voices arguing through AAC devices. A van big enough to haul all of their life saving equipment. We had to be ready for twice the chaos, twice the fear, twice the heartache, twice the hope, twice the love.

And still, even with all that, we came to the same answer: *Yes. Someone is missing.*

If God wanted us to have another child, we decided, it would happen. Carefully. Cautiously. We would get who we would get.

And then I was pregnant.

I don't know what scared me more: the thought of having another medically complex child, or the thought of having a typical one. A healthy child would grow up and go to school and bring home playground germs that could kill Lorelei. But a mito baby? That made a strange kind of sense. They'd understand each other. They could share a language of hope and pain the rest of us didn't speak. I wouldn't have to translate the way I always did for Lorelei, maybe this child would just know.

But having another child with this awful disease meant I would potentially be losing both children when they were young. It meant I would never dance with either of them at their weddings. I would never share a beer with my kid on the dock at the river. I would never be the quirky grandma from *Moana* who danced in knee-deep water as the village crazy person.

But if someone was truly missing, then maybe, just maybe, this was already written. I didn't need to grip the reins this time. That quiet voice, the one I had learned to hear, was guiding me again. And this time, I listened. I trusted that whatever was coming, we would walk through it together.

♥♥♥♥♥♥

JUST BECAUSE I was trusting that this was meant to be, did not mean I wasn't allowed to be as prepared as possible. We had no time to prepare for Hurricane Lorelei. This time, if it was necessary, we wanted to batten down the hatches as much as we were able. I mean, I had no clue how to give a typical kid Tylenol. I needed to know if this was something I *needed to know!* So we did an amniocentesis early in the pregnancy, and the first result we got was: it's a boy!

Which meant: Benji.

It was decided long before he was conceived: if we had a son, he'd carry my maiden name, Benjaminson, in nickname form. When I was a kid, my friends called me Benji, and this was my way of passing that legacy on—making him Benji, my little namesake.

Once I had basked in the joy of his name, the next wave of emotion hit. And I cried. Not just tears—full-on ugly sobs.

The emotions weren't because of the diagnosis—we didn't have that yet. They were about something simpler, and somehow harder to swallow: I didn't know how to be a Boy-Mom. I was a Disney Princess, glitter-covered, pink-sparkly kind of mama. Boys liked frogs and mud and lizards and those weird plastic snakes from the dentist's treasure box. What was I going to do with a boy?!

Many weeks later, we got the second result: he had mito, too.

My very first reaction, a combination of relief and dead-pan: "Well, I guess we don't need to worry about the pet snake."

Michael blinked. "Really?! *THAT* is your first thought?"

Benji's diagnosis didn't hit the same way Lorelei's did. It wasn't a lightning bolt of trauma. It was a quiet wave of *of course*. Surprisingly though, the grief still hit just as hard. His cells had grown slowly in the lab, something they told me wasn't necessarily diagnostic, but I knew. I knew like I always knew with Lorelei. Everything goes slower with mito. That wasn't delay. That was recognition. That was familiarity. That was history repeating itself in tiny cells.

But because of Lorelei, we knew what to do.

Because of Lorelei, we had been able to do the amniocentesis looking specifically for *FBXL4*. This was something we couldn't have done for her, because we hadn't known it was even something to look for. Because of Lorelei, the NICU team was ready for Benji. Life support equipment from the neighboring children's hospital was prepped and waiting in my c-section operating room. Mito trial drugs were flown in and were standing by. They knew the protocols. They knew the terrain. Lorelei had already drawn the map.

Benji was born one day before our scheduled c-section, after failing a final utero non-stress test. Unlike Lorelei, he made it to term. Just like before, the doula joined me in the OR, but this time, it was to help manage my anxiety and ensure that Michael could go straight to the NICU with Benji.

Despite flunking our last test together, it felt like we'd finally won something. Benji weighed six pounds, and aside from being one day early, his birth and NICU admission were... uneventful. For a few days, it felt like we'd cracked the code. I held him, breathed him in, and dared to imagine *easier*. Not normal, he still had mito and we were still in a Level IV NICU together, but maybe... lighter? Gentler? Less traumatic and far less dramatic than his sister? I imagined a version of this life that didn't come crashing down every time we exhaled.

Until Day 7.

Because the team understood the unpredictability and wide spectrum of mitochondrial disease, they ran a full assessment on Benji the day he was born. These were tests doctors wouldn't have known to run immediately if it weren't for Lorelei. Without knowledge of her and this disease, he might have initially looked like a baby with low energy and some minor feeding issues.

On Day 7, the cardiologist who had followed Lorelei for years happened to be on call. She's one of my favorite doctors. Warm, brilliant, grounded, and appreciates my sense of humor. But when she appeared at Benji's bedside wearing a very serious expression, I knew something was wrong.

She told me Benji had Hypertrophic Cardiomyopathy and Wolff-Parkinson-White Syndrome, two heart complications tied to his mitochondrial disease. The walls of his heart were thickening, leaving less room for blood to flow and less ability for it to move the way it should. His heart had changed drastically in just one week of life.

As she spoke, pieces began to fall into place. Medically, Benji looked strikingly similar to Baby Joel, another FBXL4 baby from California. Sweet Joel had only lived four months. I adored his mama and respected their story, but now I was also terrified that Benji would be gone before Christmas.

And I broke.

I cried in a way I hadn't cried since the day Lorelei was diagnosed. I couldn't stop. On Day 7, they put me on antidepressants because I was unraveling. I simply could not stop crying. Everything I'd carried for the past three years came flooding out, one tear at a time.

But even in that heartbreak, we knew what to do. Because of Lorelei.

If Benji had come first, he likely would have died without a diagnosis. We wouldn't have known what to look for, how to treat him, or what was coming. But because of her, we did. Benji lived because Lorelei lived first.

Lorelei's life wasn't just beautiful—it was *impactful*. And that's something I will never stop saying out loud. She changed the standard of care. She rewrote the playbook. She saved her brother's life before she ever held his hand.

And the things that broke me open? The sleepless nights, the medical trauma, the grief I thought might bury me... it wasn't just pain. They were all lessons in hope. They were paths of preparation.

Every appointment, every emergency, every vacation ever ruined, every gut instinct I learned to trust... It was all a crash course in surrender. In letting go of what I thought I was owed and embracing what I was given.

We don't always get to choose the curriculum, but life keeps handing us lessons anyway. The heartbreaks we didn't ask for, the chapters we wish we could rewrite, or maybe even erase. What if it is all quietly equipping us to walk someone else through the fire later?

Sometimes, life's plot twists, the ones we never wanted, become the most beautiful parts of the story. Lorelei is proof of that. And because of her, Benji lived. Every single thing we went through was leading us here.

MEANWHILE, Lorelei had zero plans to let her little brother steal the spotlight, even on his birthday.

Michael was still on the flight line, so after Benji and I failed our final non-stress test, I drove myself home, packed a bag, and got ready to head to the hospital for my c-section. As I was about to walk out the door, my mom, who was at our house taking care of Lorelei, shouted, "What do we do about rashes?"

Umm... *Excuse me?*

Cue Lorelei, stage left, ready to reclaim center.

She had broken out in a full-body rash at the exact moment I was walking out the door to have a baby. Michael rushed home and stayed with Lorelei while our hospice team came to assess the situation. Thankfully, they deemed it a fluke rash, likely nothing serious, or so we thought, and Michael made it to the hospital just in time for me to roll into surgery.

Benji spent 26 days in the NICU. And during that time, Lorelei got sick. Really sick. Inexplicably sick. The doctors tested her for everything and couldn't figure it out. Yet again she was mystifying, making no sense and playing by her own rules.

We had to divide and conquer. Michael and Grandma stayed with Lorelei. I stayed with Benji. I'd spend all day in the NICU, then come home, sobbing, walking past Lorelei to quarantine upstairs with no company other than a breast-pump. I couldn't hold her. I couldn't risk exposing Benji to whatever mystery virus she was fighting.

It was torture.

Two days before Benji came home, we finally got the answer: Mononucleosis.

MONO. The college kissing disease. What kind of after-hours frat party had my toddler been sneaking into?

Mono + mito = a nightmare. She had no energy to spare, and mono drained what little she had left. But the silver lining? They finally cleared Benji for discharge. As long as the two of them didn't share toys or play beer pong, he could come home.

And I could hold both of my children.

The first time Lorelei met Benji, it wasn't in a hospital room or perfectly posed for the 'gram. It was in our living room, cluttered with medical supplies and blanketed in exhaustion. Three of the four of us had our own pumps: his and her feeding pumps for the kids and a breast pump for me.

Lorelei sat in her Dada's lap, eyeing the tiny human curled up in mine. She studied him cautiously, unsure of who this baby was or why he was taking up her mama's attention. Benji was squeaky-crying in that absurd way only a newborn can. He sounded like a dog toy someone stepped on, and somehow, that was exactly the icebreaker Lorelei needed.

She lost it. He cried. She laughed. Full-body, belly-shaking, uncontrollable giggles.

Every time he squeaked, she laughed harder.

He squealed and wailed. She cackled and howled more.

Everyone in the room laughed and cried at the same time. It wasn't the moment I expected. But it was perfect. Because laughter and tears can sit side by side.

So can grief and joy. So can fear and love. So can labor and loss. So can heartbreak and healing. None of these cancel each other out. Instead they coexist.

We spend so much of life trying to sort the good from the bad, to separate the light from the heavy. But the truth is, they often arrive together, braided into the same moment, the same breath.

That first meeting wasn't just an introduction between siblings. It was a reminder: we are allowed to hold more than one thing at once. Two children. Two feelings. Two feeding pumps. I worried I might not have the capacity to love a second child as deeply as I loved my first. But even with all their complexities, love multiplied. I realized that hope doesn't require the absence of pain. Joy doesn't mean the grief is gone. And the most beautiful stories are rarely tidy.

Lorelei met her brother, her soulmate, her Benji, in the middle of a messy story. She decided he was hilarious and knew, without question, that he was the missing piece in our family. Just like that, they began writing their story together. For two fleeting years, their lives overlapped in one shared chapter. They were shaping each other's worlds while, once again, completely rewriting the mother—and the woman—I was becoming.

♥♥♥♥♥♥♥

Chapter 12

The Sacredest of Sacred Seasons

...when the world lived like Lorelei, for a minute.

I f I could turn back the clock to any time in the history of all time, it would be 2020.

I know, I know. I am probably the only person on the globe who would do this.

Not because life was easy. It wasn't. Lorelei still couldn't walk. Benji still couldn't eat. We were still battling the Mito Monster. Our days were built around medical care and adaptive parenting, hospital equipment, and life-stabilizing medications. My kitchen now looked like a bustling pharmacy with two kids' worth of prescriptions. My living room looked like a physical therapy clinic, complete with a revolving door of medical professionals.

But for the brief moment that was 2020, the outside world stopped spinning. And for the first time in forever, I didn't feel like we were racing to catch up.

It was also the last year that my heart was whole.

Both of my children were here. In my arms. Under my

roof. Driving me batshit crazy and making me laugh in the same five-minute span. It was hard. It was beautiful. It was quirky and rare and full of vomit.

But it was ours.

When the world shut down, people panicked. They hoarded toilet paper, googled "how long does COVID live on cardboard," became experts in disinfecting groceries, and binged *Tiger King* like it was their only responsibility. But for us, it wasn't new. It was Tuesday.

We'd been living in a world of calculated risks, hand sanitizer, masks, and a deep, constant fear of what a single virus could do, long before COVID hit the headlines. Every play-date, every doctor's appointment, every visit from a friend had always come with the question: *Is this worth the risk?* That virus fear everyone was drowning in? Our family had been swimming in it for years.

We watched as the whole world spiraled into the kind of crisis that usually only happens in Ben Affleck films with Aerosmith playing in the background. And my family was over here like, "Welcome y'all! Here's your isolation starter kit—it's made up of anxiety, Lysol, and a deep, existential fear of sniffles."

Because what changed was that, for the first time ever, in that moment, the world wasn't just looking at us with pity or confusion. They were looking *to* us. People reached out to ask how to quarantine, how to cope with the isolation, how to explain it to their kids. We became the experts. And at least in those early days, people weren't just staying home for themselves—they were staying home for *the vulnerable.* For children like Lorelei. For babies like Benji.

When it all got to be too much, people did what I'd been doing for years: embraced the dark humor, cracked jokes, sent Golden Girls memes, and found new hobbies that included, but were not limited to, sourdough baking, plant growing, and staring blankly out the window while questioning every life decision they'd ever made.

And while it didn't last—because, of course it didn't—for a moment, it felt like the world saw us. It felt like they were holding the line *with* us, not just watching from the sidelines. For a brief, shining window of time, the entire world was helping me protect my children. And that meant more than I could ever explain.

During that time of outside chaos, we had inside peace. My kids were thriving. My family was together. And telehealth became a game changer for us. The amount of time it takes to load up my children, all of their equipment, drive to the hospital for an appointment, only to sit in the waiting room for 15 minutes, risking germ exposure, see a doctor for 5 entire minutes and then go home... Thank you COVID for telehealth, and for teaching us that sometimes the sacred isn't in what we do, but instead what we stop doing.

Since we had less medical appointments, this was a period of time where I began to see my children for who they truly were. Their sibling connection. Their quirks and the things they loathed. Both of them were at a really fun age, and cognitively close despite the age gap. It was exhausting, yes, but also the best time of my life. Loud, medical, messy, and cherished.

I think that's what made it all feel so sacred, because it wasn't just that the world slowed down. It was *who* I was slowing down with. Lorelei and Benji were both in this sweet spot of connection, curiosity, and chaos. They were vibrant and weird and hilarious. And they were rare, not just medically, but in spirit. In presence. In how they took up space in a room without ever saying a word. That season wasn't just precious because it was peaceful. It was precious because *they* were. Because our disheveled, magical, loud, and laced-with-medical-jargon life wasn't just different. It was one-of-a-kind. It was rare.

♥♥♥♥♥♥♥

LET me say that again for the people in the back: it is *soooo* okay to be rare and different.

Lorelei taught us that over and over again.

And in 2020? The world was literally forced to *live like Lorelei.*

One rare disease had flipped my world upside down years earlier, canceling plans, isolating us, reshaping everything I thought motherhood would be. Then a rare virus came along and did the exact same thing to everyone else. Suddenly the entire world got a crash course in what it meant to slow down. To stay home. To rethink risk. To live without guarantees.

The world had no choice but to stop, stay still, and look around. To sit with fear. To grieve the life they thought they'd have at that moment. To find joy in the small stuff. *To live like Lorelei.*

Lorelei had been doing that all along.

She followed zero medical rules, zero social rules, and

zero beauty standards. Her face was covered in ringworm 80% of her life and she gave zero craps about it. Drooling was her jam. Loud, cartoonishly timed toots? Absolutely her favorite. She wore mismatched socks like they were designer. She side-eyed people with the precision of Jim Halpert from *The Office*. Her laugh—oh, her laugh—was the kind that could fill our whole house, always punctuated with a snort that perfectly matched the stuffed piggies we kept tucked under her arms to prop her up. It was impossible not to laugh with her.

Not once in her life did she act embarrassed about who she was. She didn't hide her face, her differences, her needs, or her joy. Maybe it was because she didn't know any different. Or maybe, just maybe, it was because she was completely at peace with herself in a way most adults will never be.

At home, my kids napped in their absurdly comfortable, camper theme printed, faux-fur dog beds on our living room floor. It wasn't for decoration, it was for practicality. Dog beds were the safest, coziest spot for two kids who couldn't sit up on their own. It kept them from rolling off a couch or a bed, and it wrapped around them like a hug. Most people saw a pet bed; Lorelei saw her throne.

We carried red Solo cups everywhere. We looked like a touring frat party, but you never knew when we'd need a "puke cup." That was our normal. So was using our kitchen fruit basket as medical-equipment storage with a feeding bag hung neatly on the banana hook, pump nestled in the basket alongside syringes and those trusty Solo cups. (You're welcome, medical mamas.) It was equal parts practical and ridiculous, which is maybe why it worked so well.

None of it felt strange to us. The dog beds, the mismatched socks, the piggie snorts, the Solo cups. They weren't quirks, they were our love language. These were the markers of our everyday life, proof that joy could be braided into the absurd and the practical.

2020 was rare in every sense of the word. Not just medically rare. Not just statistically rare. But soul-rare. The kind of rare where life feels strangely aligned, even in its mess. Where the chaos slows down just long enough for you to really *see* the people you love. Where there's nowhere to be but here, and nothing more important than a baby's giggle or the way your daughter smirks without ever saying a word.

The world was upside down, but in our little corner, we were *living like Lorelei* and it felt... almost right. We were home. We were together. We were held in this strange, beautiful in-between, where grief was out to sea for a bit, joy hadn't yet worn thin, and none of us could feel the tide shifting or the current beginning to pull at our feet. It was bliss. I had nowhere to be but with both of my children. I had nothing to do but love them.

Despite the fact that the world seemed to stop—this season didn't come with a pause button. There was no way to stretch the hours or hold them in place to remember the golden glow as sunlight hit Lorelei's curls, or Benji's fingers wrapped around mine. Time kept moving, as it always does.

If I could have bottled that season to drink it like some weirdly specific, rare grief-aged wine, I would. I didn't know it then, but I was living inside the softest goodbye. A lullaby season that was unearned, unfiltered, and absolutely ours, holding place before Lorelei's decline.

In November 2020, I took both kids to see the neurosurgeon for their routine follow-up appointment. I had no reason to believe anything was wrong. Lorelei had been fussier over the previous few months as she battled more autonomic storms, but every doctor we spoke with said it was disease progression. There were no flashing red lights. No dramatic collapse. Nothing that would have landed us in the hospital.

After we did "his and her MRIs," we were led to a quiet exam room where the doctor walked in and casually handed me the single most whiplash-inducing sentence of my life:

"The good news is Benji is being discharged from our services, but the bad news is Lorelei needs brain surgery… immediately."

Wait, I'm sorry. I beg your pardon?!

I stared at him, trying to make sense of how I could feel so high and so low in the exact same breath.

Lorelei's MRI showed her shunt, the tiny tube that drained excess fluid from her brain, had failed. Completely. The theory was that it had been failing for months, which would explain her strange symptoms and the regression everyone had been chalking up to disease progression.

But I must note here: shunts do not *usually* fail slowly over time. It is usually a dramatic failure with clear symptoms. Yet again, Lorelei baffled her audience with her latest magic trick.

I was allowed to drive the children home, drop Benji off,

and return with Lorelei for an immediate admission. At 7AM the next day, Lorelei was wheeled back to the operating room. Even though we had done this before, the feeling of signing the paperwork and handing your child over to strangers—watching the doors swing closed behind her— never, ever gets easier.

While nothing with anesthesia is uncomplicated for mito kids, this was supposed to be a straightforward procedure. In, out, new shunt, done.

Twenty minutes later, the surgeon—not a nurse, not a resident, the actual brain surgeon—walked through the waiting room doors to find us.

That is not a good sign.

There is no word, no emoji, no TikTok audio that can capture the "oh shit" feeling of seeing the neurosurgeon return before your anxiety-latte has even cooled.

"Surgery will not be happening," he said.

I still hadn't breathed yet.

"We found a golf ball-sized, pus-filled abscess in her neck."

Still not breathing.

"Brain surgery does not pair well—scratch that—brain surgery does not pair *at all* with pus."

Am I purple? Have I taken in oxygen today?

I gasped: "IS LORELEI OKAY?"

"Yes. She's okay. We removed the shunt and put in an external drain. We'll do the real surgery in two weeks and place a new shunt on the other side."

Okay. I can work with that. She is okay. We can do this.

"Also, she'll need to stay in the PICU for 14 days for IV

antibiotics. She can't go home. Actually, she can't move or even get out of bed."

Cool. Cool cool cool.

This was one of my biggest fears, having one child admitted while the other was at home. (Actually, my biggest fear was both of them being admitted at the same time, wondering if we would all share a room like one big happy mito family, but thankfully we never crossed that bridge.)

Yet again we had to divide and conquer. Benji would stay home with his home health nurse during the day, Michael would work, I would be at the PICU, and we all floated in and out of that for 14 days.

Keep in mind, this was still during the height of the COVID pandemic. We were all still terrified of catching anything, but especially the newest trending virus that could kill my children.

My mom always taught my sister and me to make an adventure out of everything. Apparently, I passed that tradition down via mitochondrial osmosis, because Lorelei never once complained. She accepted whatever came next, brain surgery mohawk for Christmas included, and made it work.

So that's what we did. We turned two brain surgeries and fourteen days in the PICU into an adventure.

That was the hospital stay where Lorelei discovered her deep, profound love for 2018's rendition of *The Grinch*. We snuggled in that godawful hospital bed and watched it so many times, the nurses started quoting it back to us.

This was also the admission where she was not metaboli-cally crashing but instead was cognitively vibrant: sassy, happy, and just the right amount of snarky, considering she was not allowed to move her head.

After so many previous admissions, the hospital staff was finally able to see Lorelei in her *real* form. She was not her usual PICU version of "dying child," but the full *Technicolor Dreamcoat* version of Lorelei: a dreamer, colorful and quirky, resilient as hell, and absolutely the lead character of her own show.

One nurse with hot pink hair and colorful tattoo sleeves became Lorelei's fast favorite. She went out of her way to bring Lorelei temporary tattoos so they could have matching sleeves, and the two bonded over their shared opinion that the 2018 Grinchy was the best—because Jim Carrey's Grinchy felt a little too terrifying. She talked to Lorelei like a child, not just a patient. Eight months later, she was still by Lorelei's bedside, as Lorelei took her last breath.

But in that moment, in that pediatric intensive care unit, we weren't waiting for joy, we were creating it. We were still holding on in the midst of our beautiful chaos. Still fighting. Still laughing. Still hoping. And for what it's worth, she rocked that double brain surgery mohawk and temporary tattoos like it was couture.

After we got home, I told myself Lorelei would bounce back to her early 2020 baseline. She always did.

But the truth was, her body was becoming more and more tired. We made it through the holiday season, but her hospitalizations started coming every other month due to metabolic crashes. Always to the PICU. Always for longer.

And I didn't see it.

I was in so deep. Deep in the feeding schedules, the

storming charts, the med logs, the suction tubes. Deep in the love. Deep in the doing. Deep in keeping both of my children alive.

I just didn't see it. Maybe I didn't want to see it. Or maybe my brain was trying to protect my heart. Or... my heart, my brain? Maybe denial is how we make space for joy when the truth is too heavy to carry.

She was slowing down, bloating up, and in more frequent pain. Grief and hope began to swirl around each other in ways I hadn't experienced before. Anticipatory grief had always been part of our journey, hovering and haunting, but this was different. This was the beginning of the end. And despite knowing the facts, I was blindsided.

Looking back, I wish I had paused more. Trusted more. Looked up more. It wouldn't have made anything easier, but it would have allowed me to be more mentally present with her.

But maybe this was the only way to carry a love this deep: by holding it so tightly you don't notice when it starts slipping through your fingers.

I had finally learned how to *live like Lorelei*, to trust, to hope, to roll with the changing tides, and to laugh at fart noises. 2020 taught me that sometimes the most sacred seasons come in the most unexpected forms.

I wish the lessons stopped there.

Because the next one was the hardest: I was about to learn how to live without Lorelei.

Chapter 13

Seven Minutes to Heaven

...lavender fields, a parking garage, and our last goodbye.

I f I could capture one day as a magical photograph and step inside it whenever I needed more time with Lorelei, it would be the day I took the kids to the lavender farm.

It was a special day in June, Benji's second birthday, and the temperature was miraculously perfect for two children who struggled to regulate their body temps. We chose this outing because it felt safe. The farm had animals for the kids to see, it was removed from crowds, tucked in the farm-fresh outdoors, away from germs that could send either of them spiraling. The kind of celebration that balanced risk and reward, where we could let them be kids without inviting catastrophe.

Rows of purple stretched out in front of us, swaying under a bright blue summer sky. The air felt crisp yet warm, with that sleepy scent that makes your shoulders drop without realizing. I laid a picnic blanket out between the rows of lavender, propping an umbrella over Lorelei. She laid on her back, tilted her head toward the breeze, her lashes fluttering as if even they were relaxing. I remember the low hum of bees somewhere nearby, the crunch of gravel under my feet, the way the sunlight caught the gold in her hair while Benji bounced in my lap.

Lorelei didn't smile wide that day. Her body was tired, and the calm of the lavender seemed to soften her even more.

That day was perfect. Magical. We were living. We soaked up the joy and stillness that comes with lying in a field of lavender, feeling the earth beneath you and the breeze above you. I didn't know it was the last time I'd see her bathed in that kind of light. I didn't know it was the last time I would go anywhere with both of my children.

We rarely know when the 'lasts' are happening; they slip by, disguised as ordinary days.

I had no idea it was our last real day of watching Lorelei live... instead of watching Lorelei die.

Within a couple of days, I realized I had caught a cold at the farm. I immediately quarantined from the kids, but it was too late. Benji, my clingy two-year-old Mama's Boy, caught it first. Then Michael.

We kept trying to isolate, but eventually Lorelei joined us on the dark side of this virus. We spent days juggling suction machines, nebulizer treatments, cough-assist machines, airway clearance vest sessions—every four hours—doing everything we could to keep their lungs clear.

This cold, which we later learned was Rhinovirus—a common cold—was Benji's very first virus, and Lorelei's very last.

She was holding her own until the perfect trifecta hit: the

virus, an autonomic storm, and the fact that it was a holiday weekend.

In true Lorelei-style, she had a knack for spending holidays in the hospital.

It was the Fourth of July, fireworks cracking in the distance, as we loaded her into the van for yet another hospital trip. I swore it would be a quick in-and-out ER visit, so to lighten the mood, we sang "Get Back Up Again" from *Trolls*—Lorelei's favorite song and our pre-hospital anthem.

I pulled into the parking garage, loaded her into her hot pink wheelchair, and headed toward the entrance of the Emergency Department. It's taken me years of therapy to understand how important that ordinary moment was.

I did what I always did: parked the van, lifted her into her wheelchair, and rolled toward the hospital doors.

What I didn't know was that those minutes at 11:45 PM —under dim yellow lights, in the humid air with that unmistakable parking-garage smell—would be precious. This was the last real moment I had with Lorelei. The last time I was truly alone with her. The last breath of fresh, albeit garage-infused, air she would take. The last moment of our normal.

Normal doesn't mean easy. Sometimes it just means familiar enough to survive. I would give anything to be back in that moment again. To pause. To hold her. To soak up that last moment of normal.

It wasn't the rest of the world's normal. It was a normal I had fought against, resented, and eventually adapted to. But I didn't know it was the last time I would live inside it with my daughter.

♥♥♥♥♥♥♥

I TRULY THOUGHT it was going to be a quick visit—a few hours in the ER, some fluids, maybe a breathing treatment, then home. Not an actual admission. But things began to fail around us—Lorelei was admitted, and sent directly to the PICU.

Michael was home with Benji. I was alone with Lorelei.

The next twenty-four hours were a blur, literally and metaphorically. I felt like I was watching *Gilmore Girls* on mute. A show I'd seen hundreds of times, so I knew what was happening, I knew what was coming—but I couldn't quite catch the witty dialogue and charming details that make it what it is.

I was watching it. Experiencing it. But not truly feeling it.

Maybe that's how our bodies protect us in times of trauma. Maybe numbness is our saving grace in moments when feeling everything might undo us completely.

Lorelei's body was crashing, and I was the mother being moved out of the PICU room with a side-arm hug from a stranger nurse while fifteen-plus people swarmed around my child to keep her alive.

There were moments in that twenty-four-hour time warp when it felt like someone unmuted it—like when the PICU attending stood over Lorelei at 4AM, after hours of trying to get an IV for the medication that would literally save her life, and mumbled, "Fuck, Lorelei. Fuck! This has to work!" And then the sound cut out again.

I've spent countless hours in EMDR trauma therapy revisiting this exact space—PICU Room 25. With the support of my incredible therapist, I'm gently guided to visualize the room. I pause the scene, feel it, experience it, try to make sense of it. I turn the volume up and down. I take in the surroundings, which usually feel like they were filmed in black and white.

I try to comprehend what actually happened. Wonder if I did enough. Wonder if I should have advocated harder... or if I should have just been more present with her, because at some point, nothing could have saved her.

So many highly trained professionals actively tried to save her, because Lorelei always bounced back. We had been here before, too many times to count. But this time was different. I knew if she was going to recover, her body just needed complete rest.

And then I demanded that the attending intubate my daughter. Immediately.

THERE WAS a respiratory therapist who pulled me aside, along with a British nurse—who I told Lorelei was Peppa Pig's Dada—and they both agreed I was a bit brazen... but I was also correct.

The RT said, "In eighteen years of doing this job, I have never seen a mom demand her daughter be intubated." Peppa's Dada added, "But you were right. You know your kid. You absolutely knew what was best for her."

Medicine and motherhood are a strange, semi-scientific

mix of data and instinct—and sometimes instinct is the only thing that matters.

She needed rest. But eventually I realized that this intubation was going to be different from Florida's. This time, there was no amount of time that I could control or give her, that would be enough for her body to bounce back.

At some point in this blur of time and hope and tears, Michael and I found ourselves in a quiet conference room, staring at a canvas wrap of stars and galaxies. I felt so small, staring at this image, while my fear and grief was all-encompassing. Everything felt different now. The air. The silence. Us.

Occasionally, fellow medical mamas ask me how I knew it was time, how I knew she was *that* tired. I don't have a clean-cut answer. I just knew.

Hope was always there, but that voice—the one that had guided me so many times throughout her journey... whether it was God, hope, or maternal intuition—was louder. And it told me the truth. If I had trusted that voice to guide me through every part of Lorelei's life, I had to trust it in her death too.

I knew Lorelei better than I've ever known another human. I knew when she needed to poop or puke, or when she needed someone to fast-forward through the commercial of the DVR'd *Frozen* movie she watched weekly... it only made sense that I would know when she wasn't going to bounce back.

But I don't think Michael knew yet. I don't think our closest family knew either. I'm not even sure if our incredible team of doctors wanted to believe it right away. Because Lorelei was always dramatic, and she *always* bounced back. But I had a feeling I couldn't shake: this was our championship game—Lorelei's Super Bowl event. We'd been training for years, and everything else had just been practice drills until this moment.

The irony is that years of planning and years of anticipatory grief didn't actually prepare me for any part of this. It had been five years since I sat in a different conference room, one floor above this one, and learned that my daughter had a rare form of mitochondrial disease. As the dark cloud of her prognosis formed above us, I started visualizing losing her. Planning her funeral. Believing that if I could plan it, I could somehow control it.

Just like everything else, I had plans for how I expected my daughter to die: at home, in our bed, with her dogs cuddled up next to her, surrounded by family, with the help of our pediatric hospice organization, and piano Disney music playing peacefully in the background. She was not supposed to die in the PICU.

Turns out, all those years of planning and anxiety didn't matter. Lorelei was going to do this how Lorelei was going to do this... and the years of anticipatory grief did not make me any more prepared to lose her.

I DIDN'T REALIZE it at the time, but on that last day, I used so many of the lessons that I learned from and with Lorelei to keep going, to make impossible choices. In the midst of making literal life-or-death decisions, I would ask myself: WWLW? *What Would Lorelei Want?*

Department heads, doctors, nurses and team members from all over the hospital stopped by our room to pay their respects and say their goodbyes. The Vascular Access Team, chaplains, residents who had been impacted by Lorelei, all came to squeeze her hand and bear hug me. We FaceTimed goodbyes to Michael's family, who couldn't make the long drive fast enough, her home health nurse, and a few of her friends, including a mito mama from Norway who had spent many nights up with me while we virtually troubleshooted our girls together.

The goodbyes were only the start to realizing the impact Lorelei made on the world around her.

Benji got one more round of sibling snuggles. We lifted him onto the bed and carefully nestled him against her side. His small body curved into hers as if he had always known that was where he belonged. He laid his hand gently on her arm, the same way he always did when he wanted to get her attention, and the hustle and bustle of the PICU faded. It was just them—brother and sister, soulmates, sharing the kind of closeness that words can't carry. I memorized the weight of it, the sight of his hair brushing against her cheek, the sound of his soft sigh, unsure why she was so sleepy.

And then, because he was still only two, because he didn't understand that the tubes and wires were holding her here, his little fingers reached curiously toward the one in her mouth. If you've ever wanted to see an entire team of medical professionals move faster than lightning, watch them when a toddler nearly extubates his sister. For a split second, the room gasped—and then, through tears, we all found ourselves laughing. The pressure valve we didn't know we needed, in the middle of the most sacred sibling goodbye.

Grandma and Papa B, Auntie Leslie and Uncle Mister were also allowed into the PICU to say goodbye, but I think they all held on to a tiny thread of hope that she would bounce back. Because that's what she *always* did.

My dad, a man of few words, most of which are typically dry and sarcastic, probably said the most impactful thing to me that day when he entered Lorelei's room. As he greeted me with the type of hug only a father can give, he said, "I'm so sorry I cannot fix this for you."

And I broke for the first time in days.

Because isn't that what all good parents want? To fix the hard, tough, broken, dark times for our children. To protect them from life's lessons that they never deserved to learn.

But love doesn't always mean fixing—it often means showing up and sitting in the brokenness together.

Michael and I spent years putting on our armor, and grabbing our weapons to battle the Mito Monster on behalf of our children. We went to mitochondrial disease conferences, we met with researchers and doctors who were experts. We also spent years making memories and living life to the fullest that this disease would allow us to live.

But no one could fix this. Any of it. Not the disease. Not the pain. Not the loss.

The same way my dad felt as he wrapped his arms around me is the way I felt a couple of hours later, as I lay snuggled in that cramped hospital bed while our favorite doctor extubated my daughter for the last time. I was grateful that I was chosen to be Lorelei's mama—so incredibly grateful. But I was also so, so devastatingly sorry I couldn't fix this for her.

♥♥♥♥♥♥♥

ON JULY 7, 2021, we were supposed to be camping for the holiday weekend, but Tropical Storm Elsa was barreling into the East Coast as Hurricane Lorelei was heading out to sea.

Just under 8 minutes after being extubated, Lorelei had a few little hiccups in my arms... and then she was gone.

On 7/7, in 7.5 minutes, she peacefully slipped away. It was our own version of Seven Minutes to Heaven, except instead of a game in a dark closet, it was a sacred stretch of time in a cramped PICU bed, my forehead resting against hers, the world narrowing to the quiet between us. The number that, in its own quiet, completed way, has always meant *whole*.

It was not what I wanted. Not what I planned for. Not where it was *supposed to be*. But it was exactly how Lorelei would have wanted it: full of love, wrapped up with Mama and Dada, and rain pouring down from a storm named after a Disney princess. It was heartbreak wrapped in beauty, a goodbye so gentle and Lorelei-perfect that even in my devastation, I knew it was a gift.

Lavender farm on Benji's second birthday.

Part Three

After Lorelei

These stories hold the woman I became—braided from grief and love, learning that survival was only the prologue. The chapters that follow are built from wreckage and wonder, each page a reminder that even broken pieces (and buckets of sarcasm) can build something beautiful.

Chapter 14

The Wake of the Storm

...breathing without her through the love, the loss and the quiet that follows.

I didn't expect to notice it—the breathing.

Not hers. Mine.

For the first time in five years, I wasn't listening for the rasp or rattle of her breath, the pause that might be too long, the alarm that might shriek at any second. The monitors were silent. The room was still. I was still.

It was an awful kind of relief, the kind you don't confess to anyone because it sounds like you wanted it. I didn't. I would have gladly stayed in that hypervigilant state forever if it meant Lorelei was still with me. But in those first few seconds, my body inhaled without bracing for disaster, and exhaled knowing she was safe, whole, and not in anymore pain.

For the first time in our entire story, I wasn't worried about Lorelei. It's jarring when the constant fear that's shaped you for years suddenly disappears. You brace for disaster out of habit, only to realize there's nothing left to guard against. That strange, aching quiet of relief mixed with guilt can feel just as heavy as the chaos ever did.

It's strange, the things you plan for—and the things you can't, the ones you could never imagine. Every vision I'd once had for typical motherhood? Gone. My adapted version of motherhood, the one I'd struggled to accept and define? Gone. The belief that Lorelei would defy the odds and outlive her prognosis? Gone. The prayers I'd whispered for years—that she would prove the doctors, the researchers, the three lonely FBXL4 case studies from 2016 wrong? Gone. Even the picture I'd carried in my head of what losing her would look like—the pre-traumatic stress visions I replayed over and over? Gone.

I wasn't wailing or collapsing the way I imagined a newly bereaved mother would. I was calm. Collected. Confused. And, in some small way, relieved. I should have remembered that there was never a right or wrong way to face this incredibly rare journey and there was not going to be a right or wrong way to handle loss either.

And then the grief truck hit me. Turned around. Mowed me down. Reversed. And ran me over again.

Considering I was a planner by nature, you'd think I would have imagined every scenario and been ready for anything. But as we rushed to the hospital three days prior, I was certain it would be another typical PICU stay. We'd been here before. We'd be home in a few days.

Now, standing in that room that sounded loudly quiet—

no machines, no beeps, just silence—someone asked if I had something for her to wear after she died. *Like... a formal ball gown?*

I dug through her gear bag—the same pastel backpack I'd hauled to admissions for years. I knew that bag by heart: every zipper, every stain from hurriedly tossed syringes or leaking formula bags. Normally, it held our survival kit—feeding tubes, medications, extra clothes, books for long waits. I'd packed and unpacked it hundreds of times, but never for this. The absurdity of reaching into it to choose the last thing she would ever wear felt like a cruel joke only hospital parents would understand. Inside, I found what was left from her Easter admission: the tie-dye dress she'd worn months earlier, a pair of white biker shorts, and an aqua hair bow that didn't match the dress at all.

So that's what she wore for her trip to the funeral home. She was a beautiful, colorful, tie-dye loving, ragamuffin. *My beautiful, colorful, tie-dye loving, ragamuffin.* And totally Lorelei.

THE STAFF SUGGESTED we leave before the funeral home arrived to pick up Lorelei—definitely before they left with her. They said it would be easier to remember her here, as she was, in her tie-dye dress with her hair pulled back perfectly. But I couldn't. I just couldn't leave her in that room. I'm not sure if I made the right decision for both me and Michael, but at that moment I was being selfish. I wasn't thinking about him. I wasn't thinking about anyone other than myself and Lorelei.

I was thinking about how I simply could not leave her in that room.

History had taught me that every time I left her alone in an intensive care unit, something went wrong. A broken femur in the NICU. The Florida crash of 2017. I wasn't going to let my last act as her mother be walking away before her body was on her way. Had they let me, I would have crammed myself into the back of the hearse to make sure she made it to the funeral home safely, too. I didn't even ask—I assumed their answer would be obvious.

If I'm being completely honest with myself, I also needed to see her body leave because I knew I would be back to the PICU one day with Benji. I couldn't carry the image of Lorelei still in that room when I returned. As difficult as it would be, I needed to see her leave. Everything in my soul needed to know she was no longer physically in that intensive care unit.

Watching her body leave that room, not in her wheelchair, was harder than watching her take her final breath.

I thought leaving Baby Lorelei in her isolette in the NICU was the hardest walk I'd ever take. I was wrong.

This time, walking out of that room, out of that building, I left with an empty wheelchair.

Its weight was ridiculous. Not physically, it was obviously lighter without her. But it was the first time I realized her absence was heavier than her body ever was. The wheels thumped against the tile hospital floor in a way they never had before, each turn reverberating down the hallway like a heavy announcement, alerting everyone within earshot that she wasn't here. Grief isn't weightless, it has mass, and in that hallway, every sound felt like it could crush me.

People glanced as we walked past their rooms, then quickly looked away. I couldn't blame them. We were living their worst nightmares. Leaving the PICU without our child, as theirs fought to survive. Life can be cruel like that: you can be the cautionary tale in one room, the brave example in another, and the whispered prayer request in the next. I've been all three.

We were frequent flyers in the hospital, and everyone knew Lorelei. I felt like we even had to comfort the security guard as we left the building with that empty pink wheelchair. Everyone knew. Everyone was hurting.

Michael and I passed through the same automatic doors we had walked through hundreds of times, but this time they didn't whoosh open into the familiar chaos of medical motherhood that always picked up after an admission. This time the doors whooshed open into something worse: a world that kept spinning without her in it.

We crossed into the parking garage in silence, the wheelchair rattling over sidewalk seams. Somewhere between the hospital doors and the car, the air changed—quieter, heavier, solemn—as if even the outside world was starting to understand she wasn't coming with us.

I don't remember much about the ride home other than asking Michael if there was anyone we needed to call or text before they saw it online. I texted Lorelei's previous nurse, who I had not spoken with in eight months. She already knew—a friend of a friend heard about it from a friend who worked in the hospital. When I say everyone knew Lorelei, I mean it was like *Six Degrees of Kevin Bacon*. Word spread, and I had no idea how, but everyone who needed to know that Lorelei earned her angel wings during a tropical storm... they knew.

Except Benji.

He adored Lorelei in the way only little brothers with the same terminal rare disease can—unconditionally, without needing her to be anything other than herself. His whole world was built around her sounds, her laugh, the rhythm of her breathing beside him.

How was I going to explain to a nonverbal two-year-old that his sister was not coming home? He had been there for his goodbye cuddles at the hospital, but I know he didn't truly understand what was happening. Even adults struggle to grasp the gravity of a goodbye before removing life support— how could Benji?

Despite his intellectual disabilities, I knew this moment would shape his world in ways we couldn't predict. Months later, after we had to put my sweet boy on anxiety medication, I realized that while we had pictures of Lorelei everywhere in the house, we didn't have any at his level, on the floor. Remembering that now makes me feel like I failed him and his grief journey. But we were all grieving and doing our best to keep going.

And so I fixed it. I lined the fireplace hearth with photos, tucked them among his toys, nestled them in the pile of plush babies he loved so much. Pictures he could see and touch. Pictures of his sister that belonged to him. Images that, I hoped, would give him comfort.

Our home is supposed to be a place that is full. Full of love and chaos and puke and medical equipment and family... and Lorelei.

As I entered my safe, not-full home, numbness set in. I walked in, set down her gear bag—where it still sits four years later as I write this, completely untouched from that day. I walk past it multiple times a day but still haven't had the strength to dig into it, fully knowing there's probably some rank, rotten article of clothing inside, not some magical love wink from my child in heaven. And then I went straight to Lorelei's dog bed.

While her human bed had been washed and completely erased any scent of her (because she puked on everything before we took her into the hospital three days prior), her dog bed still held her shape, faintly smelled like her shampoo, and was pushed up under the television in a place no one could actually see the tv from. I lowered myself into it like a scuba diver going under, curling up where she had been a few days prior, collapsing into a puddle of myself.

I didn't know yet that this was what grief would be: not one big tidal wave that takes you out in a single blow, but a series of collisions between the life that was and the life that now is. As time passed, I began to understand that the "Stages of Grief" everyone talks about were shit.

We want grief to be tidy because it makes us feel safer—like we can plan, prepare, and control it. But it isn't, and we can't. It's stormy weather on the seas: wild, unpredictable, and rarely where you expect it to be. One day grief would feel like a gentle tug of water going back out to sea, and other days it was an entire tsunami. Sometimes I would be the sailor navigating the windy seas; sometimes I would be a scuba diver using up her last liter of oxygen in the darkest depths of the ocean.

In those first hours without her, the house felt like the ocean after a hurricane: not peaceful, just unnervingly calm. The air was thick in the way it gets after a southern storm, heavy and muggy, pressing against your skin and making every breath feel like work. The storm itself had already passed, but it left behind debris you couldn't see yet.

A wake is the churn left in the water after something powerful tears through. But it is also the gathering of mourners after a life has ended. It's the moment you realize you've survived, but the world you've washed up into is unrecognizable.

The seas will rise again, the wind will return, but for now, you're left in that strange, suspended quiet... breathing, but changed forever.

Chapter 15

Grief Pie

...and the sappy, heart-welling ways we survive.

Peple have no idea how to help a family living in a chronic, medically complex life-storm. It doesn't make sense. It goes against everything we've been taught about how childhood is supposed to look. Kids are supposed to be carefree—chasing lightning bugs on summer nights, not spending those precious golden hours tethered to feeding pumps and doing bedtime respiratory treatments.

When Lorelei was alive, people knew to send support or check in when she was in the hospital. That was a crisis they understood: send coffee, drop off dinner, ask for updates. But there's no manual for the years in between, when parents are quietly drowning. Society doesn't have a grief protocol for the still-living, no handbook for how to stand beside someone whose crisis doesn't fit in a casserole dish. And it's not just medical parents—it's anyone carrying a long, quiet heartbreak: divorce, job loss, chronic illness, long-term caregiving, infertility, mental health struggles. People rally for a moment, but few know how to stay for the marathon.

Those in-between years were the hardest to explain. Like the summer she was stable enough to stay out of the hospital but not healthy enough to leave the house without calculated planning and her emergency go-bag. We'd post the occasional happy photo on social media, her outside in the sun, or Benji playing next to her, and people would comment, *It's so good to see everyone is doing so well.* What they didn't see was the night before, spent suctioning her through an airway emergency, or the 4AM med alarms we still woke up to. There was no *big emergency* to justify asking for help, so we didn't. And they didn't offer.

It's uncomfortable for those on the outside. They don't know what to say, what to do, or how to help. So often, they don't. They distance themselves, not out of cruelty, but because their lives keep going.

Their children grow and change while ours fight to simply stay here. It is an uncomfortable, widening gap to witness from both sides. From the outside, it feels awkward and helpless. From the inside, it feels like a devastating kind of survival. Caregivers grieve the skills their children lose, the jarring differences in the paths from their peers, the futures that vanish, and the community that thins out because no one knows how to sit with us in the storm.

But when someone dies? Our communities know how to rally. People bring casseroles and flowers. They send sympathy cards. They post your loved one's photo with a caption about "thoughts and prayers." It's part of the unspoken grief protocol our culture understands. This was finally a loss they recognized, a rulebook they knew by heart. Even those who only watched our life from the edges suddenly reappear, because death is a kind of tragedy they had guidelines in facing, even if they didn't want to face it.

I'd spent years learning the rules of medical motherhood —how to survive the hospital stays, the emergencies, the long nights, the short bursts of community care. I knew the parts my friends, family, and acquaintances would play, whether I liked it or not.

The day after Lorelei died, it was as if someone ripped away my hard-earned *Medically Complex Motherhood Handbook* and shoved a new one into my hands—*The Griever's Guide to the Universe*. But yet again, my version didn't match the guide everyone else was given. Theirs assumed I could collapse in bed and let the world bring soup, but mine still had caregiving duties for Benji scrawled across every page. It also came with its own set of expectations, but left out the most jarring list of all: the ordinary, ridiculous things you still have to do. Not the funeral arrangements or paperwork, you expect those. Grief rarely arrives with the luxury of pausing everything—especially for those living with chronic grief or trauma. Bills still come. Jobs still need doing. The ordinary keeps marching on. The cruelest part is how normal life insists on continuing when yours has stopped. You still have to feed the dogs. Take a shower. Arrange for strangers to collect the equipment that once kept your child alive.

Within twenty-four hours of her death, the medical equipment company called. They wanted her feeding pump back. *Immediately.* I told myself it was because another child might need it. More likely, it was because insurance stops paying when the patient is dead.

I carried it to the porch the way you carry something you never wanted to part with—carefully, reluctantly—like returning an overdue library book you loved. The pump felt heavier than it should have, as if the weight of every sleepless night was still inside it. I could still hear its soft nighttime hum in my head, that familiar click-click as it advanced, the occasional stubborn alarm that yanked me out of dreams. My fingers curled around the casing the same way they had hundreds of times in the dark, half-asleep, tracing tubing back to her.

It wasn't just a piece of plastic and circuitry—it was something I had once fought against in the NICU, convinced it meant giving up on "normal" feeding. I remember telling the head Neonatologist that Lorelei could "figure out eating with time" without a feeding tube, without a pump. As if sheer willpower could replace the calories, the time and strength she never gained. I saw it then as surrender. Now, five years later, I knew better—it wasn't surrender, it was survival.

Yet, in the end, I clung to her feeding pump with everything in me, because it had given us five years with Lorelei. This was not just medical equipment. It was a witness to our nights, our survival, our resilience. We all have totems that are ordinary to anyone else, that hold the weight of our survival stories. If there were such a thing as a hall of fame for stubborn hope, her pump deserved a spot in it. It deserved to be honored—not sitting on my pollen-covered porch like a discarded Amazon return, but on a pedestal, with a plaque that read: *This kept her here. This fed her. This gave us more time.*

I sat there watching Lorelei's pump, waiting for a stranger to take it, just like I'd waited for the funeral home to come for her at the hospital. The pump had been an extension of her body, and therefore mine—feeding her throughout the days and into the nights, clicking through its sticky buttons half-asleep at 4AM, cursing it when it alarmed for no reason. Now it sat outside, untethered from her, from me, from purpose.

When the courier walked up to my porch to take the pump that I left sitting on a small table, I wanted to look away but I also wanted to shout after him, *do you know she died? Or do you think you are just coming for an equipment exchange? Do you know what you are doing? Do you know how this is hurting me?* But he was literally just the messenger. It wasn't his fault.

Grief is weightless and crushing at the same time. Your arms ache carrying things no heavier than they were yesterday. The air presses in on your ribs. Even walking feels like dragging an invisible anchor behind you as someone is tearing away your guiding compass. But you have to keep going.

Somewhere in the haze of that day, I got a text from a friend saying I should expect a delivery. At nine o'clock that night, my Ring Camera, which earlier showed a man walking away with Lorelei's feeding pump, now showed a young girl leaving groceries on my front porch. The same table that had held the pump now held piles of pies. Every single pie the store had in stock—plus whipped cream and ice cream. At least ten pies sat, sweating under their plastic domes in the summer night air, where Lorelei's equipment had sat that morning.

It was absurd. It was beautiful. It was the first thing to make me smile since she died.

Sometimes the best grief support breaks the "rules," just like Lorelei did from day one. She never followed the medical textbook, never let the prognosis tell her what she could or couldn't do. She made her own rules, and maybe that's how we should handle grief, too.

Instead of flowers, bring something so unnecessary, so over-the-top, that it shocks the darkness for a moment. Casseroles feed the body. Pies, apparently, feed the soul. Whatever the loss, it's the wildly unnecessary acts of love that stick.

I called it *grief pie*. Pie became a staple to surviving the next few months, even if it did cause me to gain 50+ pounds down the road. But at that moment, I didn't know whether to laugh or cry, so I did both. Because grief (and pie) don't erase humor or absurdity; they just braid them together with heartbreak. It's impossible to eat around a gaping hole in your life, but it's also impossible to survive without accepting what's offered, even if it comes in the form of a pile of pies.

Everyone has their own version of grief pie. For some, it's late-night pints of ice cream after a breakup, or marathon Netflix binges when depression hits. For others, it's a ritual— baking bread, going for long runs, pouring one too many glasses of wine. We all duct tape together ways to soothe the ache no one else can see. Grief pie just happened to be mine.

There's no Hallmark card for "I'm sorry you had to give back her feeding pump." But there is Instacart and pie. And to the friends who show up for the unglamorous moments—not just the "this is what we do when someone dies" moments—you matter more than you think. You soothe in ways that can't be explained.

MEANWHILE, there was Benji.

Her feeding pump was gone, the equipment cart felt strangely empty, and yet my hands kept moving in medical-mom autopilot: checking syringes, measuring liquids, setting alarms for the middle-of-the-night doses. Most assumed that now, finally, I'd have "time" to grieve. People think grief is something you schedule. The truth is, it moves in right along-side the rest of your life and doesn't politely wait for your calendar to clear.

But my reality had doubled in weight—I had to grieve while still living in the same relentless caregiving routine. The clock didn't hand me extra hours to collapse in bed; it handed me the same schedule with half my heart missing. The contrast was cruel: the world expected me to sit in still-ness and "process," but grief didn't grant me a hall pass from the parts of my life that demanded precision and vigilance.

Society has this image of a grieving parent retreating into a quiet, candlelit room, swaddled in blankets, surrounded by casseroles, taking time to heal. That version of grief doesn't exist when you're still a medical mom. The monitors still beep. The medication schedules still dictate the day. There's no pause button—not for heartbreak, not for exhaustion, not for the blur of funeral arrangements and endless "I'm so sorry" texts. Grief doesn't pause for real life; it winds itself into the to-do list like poison ivy on a tree.

And let's not forget that Benji was still sick with the same head cold that killed his sister. He was stable and handling it like a strong two-year-old with mitochondrial disease, but he still had *the virus* that we knew had killed someone.

It was a cruel overlap—my body doing all the things it knew by heart while my mind screamed, *She's gone! He's sick!. She's gone!* It's a strange duality to be both the grieving mother and the still-active nurse. The motions that once kept two children alive now only kept one.

This is what I wish someone had told me: the world doesn't stop. Your heart stops, but the clock keeps ticking and smirking and tocking at you. And the more you wish for it to pause—the more you wish Zack Morris would step around the corner, call "TIME OUT," and freeze the chaos just long enough to look around and catch your breath—the more relentless it feels. Anyone who's lived through loss or upheaval knows that ache: life keeps marching while you're still catching your breath. You will still be asked to sign forms, return equipment, make dinner, and answer questions. You will still have to show up for someone—maybe for a living child, maybe for yourself.

Living like Lorelei means you do it. Not perfectly, not gracefully, and certainly not without tears.

Lorelei knew that better than anyone. She couldn't walk, sit up, or crawl, but when she wanted something badly enough, she'd find a way. One December, we set up the Christmas tree across the room from her dog bed—twinkling, glittering, practically shouting her name. She loved it and laid there admiring it from afar. The next morning, I walked into the living room and she was gone. My heart leapt straight to *someone had kidnapped her*—because duh, she couldn't move on her own, and that's the kind of paranoid scenario a mother's brain jumps to first.

But then I spotted her: not missing at all, just under the Christmas tree like a misplaced present, tugging on the limbs, covered in sap. Somehow, she had rolled herself like a little barrel across the entire room to get to it. Her eyes were wide and sparkling, her cheeks flushed, her fingers grabbing at the branches like she was trying to hold the whole tree in her hands. She was grinning, really grinning, the kind of joy so pure it almost hurt to look at. She looked like Cindy Lou Who herself, catching the Grinch mid-heist—not scared or confused, just utterly delighted that she'd held Christmas in her grasp. And just like the Grinch, I felt my heart swell, three sizes at least, while watching her.

I've lost count of how many times I've watched the 2018 version of *The Grinch*—first with Lorelei cuddled by my side in the PICU bed, later alone when I needed to feel close to her. There's a scene I can't unsee now, one that feels like a little love note from her every time it plays. Cindy Lou catches the Grinch dressed as Santa and, instead of asking for toys, she asks him to help her mom—because her mom works so hard, and she just wants her to be happy. Every time I hear it, I feel Lorelei whispering across the distance: *I see you, Mama. I know you've worked so hard. I just want you to be happy.* And maybe that's why I picture her under that Christmas tree—sap in her hair, light in her eyes—like she was trying to hand me my own little piece of joy, even then, a reminder to *Live Like Lorelei* when it feels impossible to keep living.

That's what survival in grief feels like. Your heart constantly aches as it grows and shrinks. You don't get there in one graceful leap—you inch, you push, you roll through the mess and the sap to get close enough to touch something that makes you feel alive again. You carry the weight of everything —the feeding pump you had to hand over like a return you never wanted to make, the pies stacked in your kitchen, both proof of love and hope in the dark season—and you keep moving toward anything that feels like light.

You might not be able to run, or even crawl, but you can still roll yourself toward the things that matter, even when it feels impossible. You have no choice but to continue showing up. You keep breathing, even when the air feels heavy. You keep moving, even when the ground feels unfamiliar. Because in grief, survival isn't about moving on—it's about moving at all.

Chapter 16

Tie-Dye Goodbye

...the most un-somber send-off ever thrown.

Before life shatters, most of us live in color: the blues in the summer sky, the pinks in a birthday cake, the way joy paints everything brighter. Then one phone call, one diagnosis, one unexpected loss, and suddenly those colors are harder to find. The world leans toward gray. You can still see the color if you fight for it, but it doesn't show up without effort.

After Lorelei's diagnosis, my world still had moments of bright, confetti-splashed magic—but they were moments I had to create, protect, and sometimes wrestle into existence. And in between, the gray lingered. Anyone who's lived through their own storms—whether it's a diagnosis, a betrayal, or a loss—knows that color doesn't just wander back in on its own, it is something you have to seek out.

Before Lorelei, my extent of medical knowledge came from *Grey's Anatomy*. Then I was forced from running my businesses, to running a PICU in my home. From crafting pages of wedding-day timelines, to color-coded medication schedules. From pitching marketing campaigns, to advocating for my kids' survival.

I traded milestone parties for quarantine, surrounded not by laughing, happy guests but by medical equipment and hospice team members. I learned how to use life-saving equipment, what to do when my child stopped breathing, and how to replace a feeding tube when the tangled dog yanked it straight out of my kid's belly.

Not long after Lorelei's diagnosis, I shut down my wedding planning business—not because I stopped loving it, but because I couldn't give my brides what they deserved. I no longer cared about seasonal color palettes, whether the mother-of-the-bride despised the mother-of-the-groom, or over which style of bridesmaids' dress the fleet of women were bickering.

My priorities didn't shift because I wanted them to, they shifted because they had to. I saw life differently after having a baby with a terminal disease. Things changed and evolved, and I learned how to act as a nurse, doctor, physical therapist, speech therapist, feeding therapist, advocate, teacher... and a mom.

Somewhere along the way, the confetti faded to ash. I used to be able to get even the shyest party guest onto the dance floor. Now, I'm terrible at parties. My life story feels like the conversational equivalent of a drunk groomsman knocking over the wedding cake during cocktail hour—except instead of fondant and frosting, I'm spilling trauma and grief all over the place.

I had always been the classic Type A overachiever: honor

code devotee, homeowner at 22, mission trip veteran, church-goer, entrepreneur with a drive to help other humans. I never litter and I have my pets spayed and neutered. On paper, perfect. I followed all the rules.

A year or so after college, I remember AOL Instant Messaging (an antique form of communicating that came after Morse Code but before iPhones) with my high school crush. In the midst of a conversation about the score of the Mets game, he told me, "I believe you are the most successful person in our graduating class. At our 20-year reunion, you will shine." I chuckled—partly because I was flattered, partly because I was blushing as if we were back in tenth-grade biology, but mostly because imposter syndrome had already taken up a long-term lease in my brain.

Twenty-ish years later, I didn't even go to our reunion. If I had, the conversation would've gone something like this:

Me: Hey, long time no see! [Uncomfortably chuckles.]

Classmate: Yeah, how's life been treating you?

Me: Well... you know... [Awkward pause.]

Classmate: [Looks around, confused.]

Me: I'm currently unemployed and trying to become a writer.

Classmate: Oh... well writing's cool. You were always good with words. Do you have kids?

Me: [Takes three gulps of wine, sets glass down, does not know what to do with my hands.] Two. They're amazing.

Classmate: I have two kids too. How old are yours?

Me: Lorelei is... dead. She'd be nine now. Benji's six.

Classmate: [Trying to quickly decide whether to cry

169

or hug me.] I'm so sorry. But at least you still have Benji. Is he starting kindergarten?

Me: No. He can't walk, talk, sit up, or eat by mouth. He's severely immunocompromised, so... yeah, no school. He has the same disease his sister had. But he's stable right now, so... huzzah? [Exhale, shrugs.]

Classmate: [Completely unsure what to say, eyes darting for escape.] Oh, hey—is that the Homecoming Queen? Hey, Suz, I'll catch you later! [Exit, stage left.]

♥♥♥♥♥♥♥

GATHERINGS BECAME UNCOMFORTABLE MINEFIELDS. You never really know how to answer "How have you been?" once life has been split into a before and after. Large crowds aren't just awkward—they're exhausting. I find myself stuck between protecting myself and my story, and protecting the people around me. No one wants me at their graduation parties, bar mitzvahs, and definitely not their baby showers. I will either bring the vibe down an entire seven levels in seven minutes, or people will treat my trauma like it's contagious.

But it goes both ways—it's also really tough for me to be around people, especially when I'm watching their kids and families thrive in their perfectly coordinated outfits, even if it did take hours of fighting to get everyone dressed. Gatherings often reopen my wounds of loss, sprinkle salt in them, and then douse them in hand sanitizer.

For years, I had gotten used to living in grayscale—long stretches of muted days interrupted by the occasional neon shock of a medical crisis. The colorful moments still existed, but they never showed up on their own. I had to hunt them down, fight for them tooth and nail, and most often build them from scratch.

And yet... the day I expected to be the hardest, gloomiest, most unbearable—Lorelei's funeral—became the most beautiful, joy-filled party I've ever thrown.

♥♥♥♥♥♥♥

WHILE I SPENT all of Lorelei's life trying to let go of planning, there was one thing I constantly thought about, despite my therapist telling me not to: her funeral. For years I planned my child's funeral, which I know, is far from normal and far from healthy. But if I had to have a daughter with a life expectancy of two-to-five years, I had to give myself grace for focusing on what I could control. And the most epic funeral possible—that was totally in my control.

I knew I did not want any part of this gathering to feel sad. This was a five year old's funeral, there was enough sadness to go around. This was a celebration of Lorelei: everything she meant to us and everything she taught us.

To avoid the overall funeral vibe, church was out. *Sorry, Jesus.* Instead, we booked a wedding venue overlooking the Chesapeake Bay. Masks were required (2021, with a fragile Benji to protect) and tie-dye was the dress code—strictly enforced by my best friends at the door with orders to turn away anyone attempting any other shade of funeral-chic.

It looked like a wedding but felt like prom: the anticipation, the hum, the undercurrent of *this is special*. And after so many months of living in and out of the PICU's grayscale, the color flooded us—spinning across dresses, swirling in the balloon garlands, dancing on the Chesapeake Bay breeze.

Despite the fact that I had been planning this for years, the minute I started booking vendors and piling party favors into my online cart, people assumed I'd spun straight into some over-the-top stage of grief. Hundreds of pinwheels? Duh! Formal tie-dye table linens? Absolutely! To everyone else, it looked like denial dressed up as event planning. But I knew exactly what we were doing: we were honoring a little girl who deserved every bit of beauty and magic this world could offer, even in death.

Despite anyone's reservations, watching my support system take on event assignments without hesitation (okay, maybe with a few eye rolls) felt like they were keeping me afloat when I needed them most.

Color spilled everywhere they worked. My friend's children placed the shimmering pinwheels along the entry sidewalks. Our doula and some NICU moms blew up hundreds of colorful balloons, turning them into a garland that wrapped the railing leading up to the ballroom. My college roommates, high school friends, and friends of my sister volunteered as tech support and photographers so those who needed to join virtually could, and so that I would have pictures and videos to hold onto later. My parents and godmothers set up mason jar centerpieces full of baby's breath and more shiny pinwheels. My sister collected hundreds of pictures of Lorelei—framing some, creating a guest book with others, and projecting them all in a slideshow at the same time. Our nurse cared for Benji in the bridal suite. One friend baked and decorated cupcakes. Another rented and manned the snow-cone machine.

It's in moments like that when you realize community isn't just about showing up for the good days—it's about holding you together on the unthinkable ones. The people who had been in the trenches with us all along showed up in force, carrying every ounce of love they had to give.

For years, I'd been chasing color—hoarding it, manufacturing it when it refused to appear. It was my rebellion against the gray, my way of insisting on light when life kept dimming around me. And then, suddenly, it was everywhere, like it had just been waiting for this day. The colors came rushing in without me having to force them. Suncatcher party favors refracted rainbows everywhere—it was the world blooming back to life in memory of Lorelei.

While setting up a banquet table full of Lorelei's trinkets —sparkly outfits, her favorite books, her fruit basket that carried her feeding pump for so many years, her Girl Scout vest with all the badges we earned together, her stuffed piggie, her acrylic light-up Christmas tree, and so many other things that belonged to her—I stood in awe, watching people who loved me, who loved Lorelei, come together to make this celebration magical.

I had spent years feeling isolated and alone on this journey, but the day of Lorelei's funeral was akin to the final scene from *Encanto*, when everyone in town reminds the family to lay down their load, singing, that they have no gifts but as a group they are many, and that they will do anything for you.

My vision, that this event would be anything but a

somber, black-clothes-and-hushed-condolences gathering, came to fruition. Lorelei's life was technicolor. She deserved a tie-dye, technicolor goodbye.

The ballroom was filled with every corner of her world—family, friends, doctors, nurses, therapists, strangers-turned-friends from the internet. Two pastors, one being the chaplain from the hospital, preached in white gowns with custom tie-dye stoles. The geneticist who diagnosed her spoke. My sister and college roommate offered welcomes and prayers.

Then it was my turn. Fingers gripping the podium, I felt far less chill than my tie-dye dress suggested. I shared the eulogy I'd written at 4AM, *Lessons from Lorelei*—not like it was a checklist, but like it was our gospel. Somewhere between "Do not take your calendar too seriously" and "A hammock is never a bad idea," people started laughing through tears, nodding, and weaving her lessons into their own lives. I realized Lorelei's story wasn't just mine to carry anymore—it belonged to every single person in that room.

When I finished, music swelled and kids twirled on the dance floor. Guests swarmed me for copies of the lessons, swearing I had to make them into a book.

Every guest left what was supposed to be an all-encompassing, universally known grief-fest feeling lighter, brighter, and more determined to live Lorelei's lessons to their fullest. And as they hugged me goodbye, I caught whiffs of lavender and cupcakes—a technicolor kind of proof that Lorelei was everywhere at once, soaking up every glimmer of this day with us.

The salty air was heavy with a bittersweet mix of joy and ache that only exists when love and loss share the same space.

When the music faded and the last guests stepped out into the evening, I stood in the quiet, watching the sunset on the bay, holding onto that warmth like a lifeline. In the end, that's what we're all chasing—the moments that remind us we're still here, still connected, still able to feel something other than the weight.

Grief can be dark. But it can also be bold, bright, and colorful. That day, I learned that sometimes the color that's been missing, that you've been chasing all along, can flood back in on its own, or with the help of your support system—and when it does, you let it wash over you.

Photo Credit: Katie Wilson Photography

Chapter 17

Look Up, Mama

...when the sky looks different.

N ot long after Lorelei died, I stepped outside into a world that was both familiar and entirely altered. I sat on the steps of my back deck, staring out at our backyard, the empty swing-set, and her vacant She Shed. Coffee in my hand, hot July air on my skin. Tropical Storm Elsa had moved out into the Atlantic, and Hurricane Lorelei had taken half my heart with her.

As an East Coast girl, I've faced my share of hurricanes. There's something about the sky afterward—that first glimpse of blue and sunshine breaking through the gray—that always catches me off guard. The debris and snapped branches remain, but the light feels sharper, almost holy.

That morning was no different. The air was the same temperature. The clouds floated where they always floated. The sun rose in its usual place, spilling early-morning colors across the horizon. And yet... the sky looked different.

That's what grief feels like. Debris is everywhere—sharp,

messy, muddy, and impossible to clear in a day. You stumble over it when you least expect it. And somehow, light filters through the wreckage, catching on jagged edges, making the broken things glow while shadows stretch long. The hurricane doesn't erase what was lost, but it leaves behind a landscape where grief and hope sit side by side.

Maybe it was a reflection of my heart. Maybe it was the after-hurricane glow. But it wasn't anything you could measure with instruments or explain in weather terminology. The entire canvas of the world had shifted—the same view, repainted in a way only I could see. It felt like the veil between here and heaven had thinned, just enough for me to recognize her presence on the other side.

I had spent five years looking at that sky with Lorelei beneath it, breathing the same air, living under the same technicolor ceiling of blue and gray and pink and gold. Now she was gone, but somehow, she was still here. The physical emptiness was vast, but I could feel her with me in a way I'd never experienced before—as if she were filling the very sky around me.

I used to believe Heaven was some far-off, unreachable place. But under that sky, I felt the truth: Heaven is closer than we think, and our angels, ancestors, and loved ones are still with us—just in a different form. Heaven isn't 'up there.' It's here, stitched into the air we breathe. It isn't somewhere our souls travel to; it's a presence that travels with us.

In that moment, I felt like Lorelei had taken on the caregiver role, and I was her baby. For years, I had been the one keeping her safe, pouring whatever magic I could into her life. But now she was the one watching over me—keeping me safe, reminding me I am loved, leading me toward whatever bits of magic she might find.

I had always assumed that when someone dies, your relationship with them ends. Before Lorelei, I had only lost grandparents, and I kept them alive only through memories. But losing her taught me something different: my relationship with my daughter had not ended. It had simply changed. We were—and still are—connected, just in a different way.

I struggle when people ask me how old my kids are. A lot of bereaved moms use descriptions like "forever five," and that's totally okay, but it doesn't feel quite right for me. Lorelei isn't frozen in time. In my mind's eye she sometimes looks five, sometimes a toddler, sometimes even a baby—but always my Lorelei. She keeps aging though, because I've known her spirit since 2016, and her soul hasn't stopped growing.

I've been parenting her for years beyond her body, but in so many ways she's been parenting me too. Our relationship didn't quit when her mitochondria finally quit—it shifted. She continues to show me who she is becoming, and just as much, she continues to show me who I can still become.

♥♥♥♥♥♥

THE SILENCE of the sky was broken by the buzz of my phone in my pocket. Oddly, the days after someone dies—when you only want to talk to one person, the one you can't—your phone doesn't stop ringing. There are calls to make, calls to take, and more conversations than you can process. I found it easier to pace up-and-down the deck as I talked, letting the motion steady me.

Mid-sentence, on a call with Lorelei's home health nurse, my eyes dropped to the boards beneath my feet. That's when I saw it—a heart, perfectly formed in the grain of the wood. How many times had I walked this deck and never noticed? And yet, here it was. I hadn't gone looking for it; it was simply there, waiting. My first *Love Wink from Lorelei*.

At first, I didn't know what to make of it. Was it a coincidence? A trick of the light? People might think I was imagining things—but the warmth blooming in my chest told me it was her. It felt like a quiet, familiar, visual message from my nonverbal child: *I'm still here, Mama. I'm still here.*

That heart became our new way of speaking, a thread between us. It showed up on the hard days, but also on the beautiful ones. On beach walks with my heaven-based daughter, I'd spot heart-shaped seashells, proof we could still do things together. In the foam of my morning coffee, a single heart-shaped bubble would surface, reassuring me we were still starting our days, somehow, in sync. A tiny heart in Benji's food, blended for his feeding tube, confirmation that she was still looking out for her little brother.

These signs, that I call love winks, are not proof so much as permission. Permission to believe we're still connected, permission to notice what we might otherwise dismiss, permission to keep the conversation going with the ones we love.

I began sharing these signs on social media, and before long, #LoveWinksFromLorelei belonged to everyone. Friends and family started sending me photos: a heart-shaped cloud, a spill on the counter, a leaf on the sidewalk, even a chicken nugget. Kids would tell their parents "Lorelei is with us! Send this to Lorelei's mama!" when they spotted a heart on the playground. One night, long after I'd gone to bed, a photo lit up my phone: a potato, perfectly heart-shaped, with the caption, *"Potato Love Wink from Lorelei—she says hi, Mama!"*

Lorelei continues to take creative liberties with communication. One minute she's a sunset sky and rainbows, the next she's a potato in someone's pantry. Of course she'd refuse to pick between sacred and ridiculous. Love shows up how and where it wants, holy and hilarious, daring us to stay open.

Some people sent me one or two Love Winks. Others sent dozens over the years. And then there's my friend Katherine who continues to take it to the next level. Katherine and I haven't talked regularly since college, but we've always known we're one quick text away if either of us needed something. She lives on the opposite side of the country and had never met Lorelei, yet to this day—years after Lorelei passed—Katherine sends me more #LoveWinks-FromLorelei than anyone else.

One day she asked me, "Why do you think Lorelei sends me so many love winks when I never met her?" I told her I think it's because Lorelei knew Katherine would not only be open to noticing them, but that she would text me every single time—even when I was too griefy to respond.

The further away we get from losing someone, the more they tend to fade from other people's everyday thoughts. I remember Lorelei every single day. She's my first thought when I wake up and my last goodnight before I sleep—but

I'm her mama. I don't expect the rest of the world to carry her with them the same way.

So when someone goes out of their way not only to think about my girl, but to tell me about the love wink they saw, or better yet, the memory they had of her, it's another way of keeping her close. It's a connection, not just between me and that person, but between me and Lorelei.

Over time, I realized it was even bigger than tiny hidden hearts. Lorelei's love was multiplying, not shrinking. People who had never met her were seeing love winks that reminded them of *their* people, too. Bumblebees connected my friend to her dad. A cardinal made them think of a grandmother. Colorful scarves brought back a sibling. A crown connected a mother to her son. Lorelei's love wasn't just rippling out—it was cross-pollinating, opening people up to the idea that the ones we love are still here with us, just in a different form.

HEARTS AREN'T the only way Lorelei has stayed connected. At her funeral, we gave suncatchers to our guests as party favors—small circles of glass meant to refract rainbows across the room when the light hit just right. I wanted people to take a little bit of Lorelei's color home with them, a reminder that she was more than the dark disease that dictated her life. She was joy and light and wild, impossible magic. But I also wanted them to remember that grief doesn't have to be dark. It can shimmer. It can be colorful.

Because so many people joined her funeral remotely, we

also mailed suncatchers to friends around the world. It wasn't long before messages started rolling in:

"The sun came through my kitchen window today and there were rainbows all over my fridge. I knew she was here."

"The rainbows hit my baby's crib this morning. Lorelei's looking out for us."

"Lorelei had rainbows all over the stairwell as I was preparing to head into work on a really big meeting!"

Her rainbows have shown up in houses, offices, and hospital rooms—in the USA, Norway, Switzerland, Canada, and even Australia. Places she never physically touched but somehow still manages to fill. There's a strange kind of math to grief: her body isn't here, yet her presence is everywhere.

My friend Jeni is a psychic medium. In the middle of a casual conversation, she suddenly stopped, tears welling in her eyes—something I had never seen happen to her before. She told me she was receiving a download from Lorelei. Usually when Jeni connects with spirits, it's through feelings or words. But Lorelei communicates by showing Jeni blocks of pictures.

At that moment, I had just been telling Jeni how deeply I missed my girl, how my grief felt like I was wearing a heavy, soaking-wet Snuggie that was weighing me down and preventing me from connecting with Lorelei the way I desperately longed to. And in response, Lorelei decided to show Jeni the opposite: beauty, peace, safety, sacredness. She was trying to *visually* describe what Heaven looked like. In all Jeni's years of connecting with spirits, Lorelei was the first to try to paint a picture of Heaven, like the sun colors the sky at sunrise—because of course it would be my sassy, colorful little girl who wanted to make sure everyone knew just how bright it is on the other side.

More than that, though, Lorelei wanted her mama to know she was okay. That even if I couldn't feel her the way I wanted to, she was safe. She was loved. She was still with me. And because she was okay, I could loosen my grip on the grief I was carrying. I could take off a few of those heavy, suffocating layers I'd been wearing—because she wasn't lost, she had only changed form.

That mindset shift didn't erase my grief, but it made space inside it. Space to breathe. Space to begin noticing slivers of colors in rainbows again. Space to imagine that maybe, just maybe, I could find myself again, too.

The quiet morning sky that felt different, it was my first lesson in this new version of our relationship. She's not here in the way I want her to be, but she's still mine, and I'm still hers. She finds me in hearts and rainbows and the occasional potato. She finds her way into the lives of people she never met, threading herself into their stories like she has always been there.

One of Lorelei's hype songs on tough days was Lauren Daigle's *Look Up Child*. It begins in darkness, questioning where God is when the world feels broken, but always circles back to the reminder to lift your eyes. To look up. When I look up now, I don't just see sun-streaked skies—I see the thin place where here and there meet. And when I look down, I see her love etched into wood, scattered across the floor in tiny rainbows, or shaped into a leaf resting in my driveway.

Maybe that's the point of it all—not whether the sign was "real" or not, but that it made me look up. Grief tempts us to close off, to shrink down, to stop noticing. Signs dare us to stay awake to beauty, to absurdity, to love that hasn't gone anywhere.

The sky looks different because I am different. I am still her mother, just in a relationship that defies geography. And every time I catch one of her love winks, I remember: love doesn't disappear. It just changes form. Some call it angels, some call it signs, some call it the thin veil between worlds. I call it Lorelei—still my girl, still loving me, still teaching me to look up.

♥♥♥♥♥♥♥

Chapter 18

Apricity

...the warmth of the sun in the winter.

One of the incredible co-hostesses on my podcast *When Autumn Comes*, Diane, always says that two things can sit together at the same time without blending into each other. For many years of podcasting together, I always agreed with her—nodding along, hearing what she said—but not really understanding what she meant.

When Lorelei died, it was the first time I truly felt what it meant to hold two opposite things at the same exact time. The moment Lorelei took her last breath, I was hit with two completely contradictory emotions at once: grief and relief. My daughter was gone from me, and my daughter was free from mitochondrial disease. Both realities lived in me, side by side, neither one canceling out the other.

That was *apricity*. I didn't know the word then, but I knew the feeling: warmth piercing through unbearable cold.

It's like missing the quiet while craving company, or loving a person deeply while being utterly exasperated by them. It's laughing at a funeral and crying during a wedding toast. The paradox isn't rare—it's daily.

With time, and plenty of grief pie, I realized what Diane truly meant, and I understood that I had been living this strange paradox for years as a caregiver:

Feeling the sadness of the disease, but also the beauty of my children.

The grind of medical caregiving, but the joy of milestones we were told would never come.

The fear of tomorrow, but the presence of today.

I had been experiencing apricity all along. I just didn't have the language, or the capacity to truly grasp what that meant, until I lost her.

I see it most clearly in how I mother Benji. With Lorelei, I spent so much of her life pushing: therapies, exercises, endless hours of trying to prove science wrong. It came from love, but also from desperation. The desperation of a mother who wanted the impossible. I wanted her stronger, better, longer.

With Benji, I don't push in the same way. I let him be himself. I let us breathe. Maybe it looks like I've lowered the bar, but in reality, I finally understand what the bar is for: not to measure what my kids can accomplish, but to hold space for who they already are.

I would cut off my right arm with a dull, rusty butter knife if it meant I could cuddle Lorelei for just five more seconds. Grief makes you bargain in absurd, impossible ways. All those days I spent with her when I wasn't actually present: when I was scouring the internet for trial medications and research labs that would study FBXL4, when I was trying so hard to get her to eat by mouth, when I followed the cry-it-out method because that's what the pediatrician said to do, when I was trying to fix her instead of simply letting her be her.

But, if given the opportunity, grief can also become a guide that helps us navigate the "because ofs" rather than the "what ifs" of our experiences.

Because of Lorelei, I am a better mom for Benji. More present. More grounded. More willing to love him right where he is, without needing him to prove anyone wrong.

Because of Lorelei—and Benji—my life changed in ways I never saw coming. I stumbled into a whole world of scrappy, resilient caregiving parents who were fighting similar invisible battles. We all ended up in this caregiving community from different walks of life. Everyone has different backgrounds and different diseases or conditions that caused our lives to implode, but we all share the same feelings of heavy loss and anticipatory grief, paired with unwavering love and hope. I found people who spoke my language without needing translation.

In 2022, with the help of my support system, I created The Apricity Hope Project as a way to bring warmth into winters like mine. This nonprofit organization became a gathering place for weary caregivers—wrapping them in a metaphorical blanket during their coldest, darkest seasons, reminding them that they are not alone.

The Apricity Hope Project provides mental, physical, and emotional health support for moms and dads of medically complex, disabled children. It exists so they can show up as parents at their fullest capacity—not only as caregivers. It exists so they don't drown in medical life, and so they don't miss the opportunity to be present with their children.

Because of Lorelei, I knew there was light even in the winter.

Because of my village—the people who carried me when Lorelei and I were in and out of the PICU, and then when I was grieving her loss—I knew how invaluable community support truly was.

When the *what ifs* sneak into my mind—What if she had been healthy? What if her disease hadn't been mitochondrial disease, but something more manageable? What if she had not died?—I remind myself of the *because ofs* and all the light that has come my way because of Lorelei.

Because of Lorelei, I learned what resilience and strength truly mean.

Because of Lorelei, I met incredible people whose paths I never would have crossed otherwise.

Because of Lorelei, I discovered a passion for helping people and a gift for creating spaces that allowed souls to breathe again.

Because of Lorelei, I learned my creativity could serve a purpose far bigger than myself.

Because of Lorelei, I realized that I, too, had magic inside of me.

♥♥♥♥♥♥♥

IT IS OFTEN ASSUMED that I created The Apricity Hope Project in honor of Lorelei. While she is part of my daily inspiration to manage, create, and *live like Lorelei* through this organization, she was not the original inspiration for this nonprofit.

I created AHP in honor of the version of me who sat in the NICU conference room when a team of doctors delivered earth-shattering news. The version of me who sat next to the isolette in the dim NICU, when everyone around me seemed to be speaking a language I couldn't speak or understand. The version of me who found herself tethered to a breast pump, crying, because this was not what I expected motherhood to look like. The version of me who watched her friends raise typical kids that were meeting milestones, while my baby couldn't hold her head up.

I created The Apricity Hope Project for the women who need support during their darkest moments, hoping and praying it would somehow give them the love, encouragement, and strength to remember that they are bright, brilliant, fun women—not just caregivers living under the shadow of a dark, cloudy diagnosis. It wasn't just about surviving anymore; it was about remembering who we were outside of caregiving.

What surprised me most in building AHP was how much I came alive in the process. In building a space for other caregivers, I uncovered a part of myself I thought had been buried under medical charts and sleepless nights. I was able to dust off my event-planning and entrepreneurial skills I hadn't touched in years. When I closed my wedding business, it was because I could no longer connect with, or sincerely serve, my brides. But fellow caregiving moms who were stuck in the darkness I was slowly finding my way out of... I was here for them.

Between the diagnoses and the losses, the long nights and exhausting days, the trauma and the heartache, I had become a hypervigilant, anxious, depressed version of myself. Always scanning for danger. Always bracing for the next collapse. And while those pieces of me—the anxious one, the protective one, the exhausted-but-determined one—will always be part of who I am, I've learned they don't have to define the whole story.

Through Lorelei's loss, and a lot of trauma therapy, I realized all these parts of me can coexist. They don't cancel each other out. They shine when they're needed. Even the pieces I used to wish away—the anxious, the hypervigilant, the exhausted—weren't bad parts. They were just trying to protect me.

As I learned more about myself, I realized I could thank all the versions of me, and all my protective parts, while letting other parts breathe again. Lorelei never seemed to question herself... she lived in full color, unfiltered, exactly as she was. Maybe she was just teaching me how to do the same: to embrace all the parts and still live as my truest self—creative, playful, hopeful—and Benji and Lorelei's mama.

WHILE I EMBRACED many of my layers, I also found myself searching for the ones I had lost along the way. I wanted to remember what my true self loved, what still made me feel alive in the middle of all the heaviness. I was deeply entrenched in Benji's lifesaving care, but if what I was teaching my community was true—that caring for yourself makes you a better caregiver—then I had to believe I would be a better mom to my son if I was also a kinder person to myself.

Before Lorelei died, the only time I had picked up a paintbrush was in elementary school. But one day, my never-wrong internal voice told me I needed to paint. Paint what? I had no clue. But laying in Lorelei's bed, I grief-purchased all the supplies, knowing I just needed to sit down and see what would happen. In Lorelei's She Shed I started blending colors across a canvas and painting my first *Stars for Benji* piece. I loved that there were no life-or-death decisions in art, only color and possibility, and I firmly believed I could make anything pretty. Maybe for someone else, it's gardening or running marathons, but for me, it turned out to be a paintbrush.

In that quiet, messy act of creating, my brain finally calmed down. I felt connected not only to Lorelei, but to a colorful version of myself I didn't know existed. What started as one canvas turned into hundreds of *Stars for Benji* paintings, sold to raise money for mitochondrial disease research. Art showed me that I could still create beauty in the middle of chaos, and that I could find pieces of myself I thought had been lost forever. That realization opened the door to another part of me I had buried: my love of travel.

Before my kids, I traveled—a lot. Travel wasn't just a hobby; it was woven into me. It was what brought my family closer when I was growing up, and it was one of the funda-mental joys my husband and I shared when we first built our life together. But with both kids severely immunocompromised, and neither of them able to pack lightly with all their medical equipment, I convinced myself that the wanderlust version of me was gone.

Reaching back to find myself, I discovered I could still travel. It began in 2017, after Lorelei survived the flu and I was a shell of myself. My high school bestie, Jess, and I planned a trip to Key West. She was endlessly patient as I struggled to unplug from caregiving. Reminding myself that Lorelei was safe at home with Michael, and *only* a sixteen-hour car ride away if there was an emergency, I let Jess lead me toward rest.

With the help of copious piña coladas and too many slices of key lime pie, I discovered that clear, salt water on Key West sandbars soothes my soul in ways I can't explain. Allowing myself to lie in two inches of turquoise water on a private sandbar with no cell service and no other humans was terrifying, but it fed my soul, silenced the anxious parts of me, and reminded me of who I really was.

We all need our sandbars, the quiet places that anchor and remind us who we are when the world drowns us. For me, it became an annual pilgrimage to the turquoise shallows —those picturesque sandbars where a local boat captain named Ally would drop anchor—to reconnect with my true self and remember that I was still alive, too.

As I grew braver, I still kept one boundary for myself: I couldn't travel anywhere I couldn't drive home from. But a little over a year after Lorelei died, on a whim, I decided not only that I wanted to go beyond that boundary—but that I *needed* to. To Norway. To finally meet Lorelei's mito soul sister, Nea, and her mama, my own soul sister, Gunhild.

I remember walking into our garage where Michael was working and blurting, "Hey, can I go to Norway?"

Michael looked up and said, "Sure, I don't see why not. One day?"

I replied, "I was actually thinking about going next week... I found a really inexpensive flight."

Michael, shocked but remembering how I used to travel the world, said, "I don't have a problem with it, but are you sure *you* can handle it? Benji is stable right now, but you do realize that you can't drive home from Norway... right?"

I booked the ticket immediately and crossed the ocean a few days later to meet strangers who already felt like family. Gunhild and I had spent countless hours talking about our girls (and later Benji) as we navigated a disease no one seemed to understand. While FBXL4 kids vary in presentation, our children could have been siblings: physically, medically, even in their quirks.

I was nervous—not about the distance, the language barrier, or even meeting people I'd never hugged before. I was terrified because this was my first big trip since Lorelei died. What if I couldn't feel her with me outside of our home? What if she was only where she had lived her whole life, and not in the wide world?

But on the flight, I felt her. In the quiet mornings in a little Norwegian waterfront apartment, I felt her. Hugging sweet Nea, I felt her. And when I hiked seven hours to the top of Pulpit Rock, lungs burning and heart aching, inches from potentially slipping, falling, and plummeting to my death, I felt her with me every single step. Norway was the first time I realized I could be both: more like my old self, while still fully my new self. Which is the ultimate paradox of loss: we don't go back to who we were; we learn to carry them alongside who we are becoming. And in Norway, carrying her felt less like grief and more like companionship. It was as if I had finally taken Lorelei on a mother-daughter trip—the kind we never got to have—chasing Ana and Elsa through the fjords, because she was everywhere with me.

That impulsive trip, booked with only five days' notice, reminded me that I was still capable of chasing awe and that Lorelei would always be with me. But it also taught me I didn't want to miss opportunities with Benji while he was here.

So we sold our big family RV and bought a small campervan I could handle on my own when Michael isn't able to join us. The goal was simple: a safe, germ-controlled space for him, a bed for diaper changes when the world doesn't accommodate kids like mine, and something that was ours. Now we take small "Mama+Bear adVANture" road trips—weekend camping trips that feel like our own version of freedom. Freedom together. Freedom from the suffocating monotony of medical life. Freedom from the reality of his disease. Freedom to make memories with my son.

These became my forms of apricity: painting, traveling, salt water, campervan weekends with my boy. My ways of bringing warmth into a heavy, dark season where his disease is visibly progressing. Proof that even winters have colorful moments and unexpected hope.

♥♥♥♥♥♥♥

As hope rippled through the caregiving community, the Apricity Hope Project grew faster than any of us expected. The need for caregiver support was so great that my board of directors and I were staring down our five-year goals only eight months in.

We had planned for a headquarters that could double as a retreat house somewhere down the line. But it became clear right away: if we wanted to make the biggest impact, we needed a place now. A space that felt safe, welcoming, and designed for parents—a refuge beyond the walls of the hospital.

Taking on a property felt enormous—and terrifying—for such a young organization. Financially, it made no sense, and half my board was quick to remind me of the risks. They weren't wrong. Still, I couldn't shake the sense that we were being pulled toward something bigger. So I asked Lorelei to show me a sign if this was supposed to happen. I expected a small love wink from her. Instead, a hot pink house on the water overlooking the bay appeared for rent. My mom, who happened to be our Realtor, called the listing agent—a friend she'd known for over forty years—and within hours of it hitting the market, we were walking through the house ourselves.

I could feel an energy from this place, beyond its pink walls. It felt like Lorelei had picked it out just for us. Just for the mamas and dadas who needed it. The first time I went into the house that would soon become the Apricity Hideaway, I wasn't sure what I was looking for. But as I walked into the living room, moments before sunset, the light hit a decorative table just right—hundreds of rainbow prisms scattered color across the walls, fragments of brightness in every corner.

It felt like Lorelei's fingerprints. Her way of saying, *Yes, Mama. This is it. This is where you will braid all the things you love—colors, art, event planning, and salt water—and find yourself while helping others. This is where you'll bring moms and dads to feel the sun in their own winters.*

The Apricity Hideaway became more than a space for retreats; it became a reflection of my own self-discovery. I wasn't just building a refuge for others—I was building one for myself. A place where I could grieve and create. A place where I could be both a mother and a woman. A place where I could remember who I was and who I was still becoming.

Apricity is the word for what I'm learning to do: carry the frost and the warmth together. To stop waiting for the cold to end, and instead, allow the sun on my face to remind me I can still live.

The *what ifs* will always ache. But the *because ofs* carry me forward.

Because of Lorelei, I am a better mother.

Because of Lorelei, I am a truer version of myself.

Because of Lorelei, I carry warmth into the cold.

Grief will always be winter. But because of her, the sun still finds my face.

♥♥♥♥♥♥♥

Norway Trip –
Pulpit Rock with Gunhild

Key West Sandbar

AdVANtures with Benji
in the campervan

Apricity Hideaway,
Norfolk, VA

Chapter 19

The Story Worth Telling

...the way my daughter taught me to live my own story.

I used to think life was a straight path. If I followed the rules, checked the boxes, did everything *right*, I would land exactly where I was *supposed* to be. It felt almost guaranteed: hard work plus good choices equaled safe outcomes.

But then Lorelei came, and burned the map, shattered the GPS, and tossed my compass into the sea like the old lady at the end of *Titanic*.

The path I thought I was on disappeared, replaced by one I never knew existed: hospital rooms, medical acronyms, caregiving detours. And yet—even there, even in the hardest seasons—I was exactly where I was meant to be.

The truth is, life is not linear. It's a book of chapters, each one shaping the story in its own way. It is seasons. It is pivots. It is lessons that keep teaching us—and Lorelei was my best teacher.

She never followed a script. She ignored milestones, rewrote expectations, and carried genetics that made no scientific sense. She reminded me that a magical life rarely makes sense either. She laughed at the wrong times, snorted mid-giggle, and broke every rule about how a little girl was supposed to behave. She lived unapologetically her way—and in doing so, she gave me permission to live that way too.

It took a five-year-old who couldn't speak to turn me into the woman writing these words. Every ounce of strength I have, every laugh I've learned to let out, every prayer I still whisper when I'm scared—it all traces back to her.

I have experienced some pretty incredible chapters. But I have also lived through dark chapters I never expected to face, and others I would completely skip if given the opportunity.

Motherhood chapters: from baby showers to NICU monitors, from vacation plans to vacations canceled, from working mom to stay-at-home nurse. Motherhood wasn't what I pictured, but it was still motherhood—just written in a language I never expected to learn.

Identity chapters: from busy entrepreneur, to isolated and anxious medical mom, to hopeful nonprofit founder. At first, every version of me felt like a loss, but each one carried me closer to the woman I was becoming.

Grief chapters: diagnosis day, the day Lorelei died, when the entire story shifted again without my permission. Grief rewrote me in ways nothing else could—painful, yes, but also proof that love leaves an imprint deep enough to change you forever.

Each of these chapters felt like a traumatic rupture at first, as though I had failed the story I believed I was writing. They weren't the chapters I dreamed of, but they wrote me into who I am. Looking back, I see they weren't failures at all. They were plot twists that gave my story its depth, texture, and weight. Without them, it would have been a flat, unfinished draft.

And maybe that's the point of chapters: they don't just move the story forward, they change the narrator along the way. They sharpen what we know about ourselves. They reveal strengths we didn't think we had. They turn detours into direction.

We all have them. The chapters we'd rather rip out of the book. The ones that drag on too long, or end before we're ready. The ones that make no sense until years later, when you finally see how they connect to the story as a whole.

If only life worked like those old *Choose Your Own Adventure* books, where you could peek at the ending, flip back a few pages, and pick the path that guaranteed the outcome you want. But real life doesn't offer page numbers to skip ahead. It throws you unexpected twists and dares you to keep going. Courage doesn't come from knowing the ending —it comes from turning the page anyway. There's no flipping back to rewrite the story or skipping ahead to see if things turn out okay. You only get this page, this choice, this moment —and somehow, that has to be enough.

As I sit here writing, cozied up in my bed, with Benji's left arm hooked into my right arm, listening to him softly breathe next to me... I am in awe of how all of the previous chapters got me here, with this sweet boy wrapped around me. Our previous chapters were not easy, and as his disease progresses, I know our future chapters will include more pain and loss. But I'm beyond grateful to be here in this moment right now. This is the chapter I am in now, and even with all of its exhaustion and ache, it's still beautiful.

Sometimes the chapters are sacred and magical, like Norway on five days' notice, or lavender farms in the sunshine. Sometimes they are dark and devastating, like diagnoses, brain surgeries, or death. But just like the seasons of the year, none of these chapters last forever. Neither the good nor the bad.

Some chapters drag on longer than you'd like. Some slam shut without warning. Some sparkle so brightly you wish they could last forever. But every single one belongs to the same book. My book.

Recall the woman you met in Part One of this book, the one with the plans and the goals, the one who thought she knew what was hard... Oh, bless her sweet and innocent heart. Because hard is always about perspective. Back then, her definition of hard was real. She was navigating a new diagnosis, a body that betrayed her pregnancy, and a future she didn't see coming. It was overwhelming, confusing, and heavy. But she couldn't have known the difficult times that were still ahead—the nights of managing two medically complex kids, the endless alarms, the constant fear. And she definitely couldn't have fathomed the hardest of all: life without Lorelei here.

Perspective has a way of showing us what once felt impossible might now look survivable, and what feels unbearable today may one day soften. Time doesn't erase pain, but it can transform its meaning. Each chapter doesn't just rewrite how we see the world, it redefines what love and hope can make possible.

Lorelei shifted my perspective in countless ways. She taught me to trust when nothing made sense. To laugh when the storm raged. To belong without apology. To be present in the moment I had, not the one I thought was coming. She taught me to live unscripted, giving me permission to keep turning the page, no matter how jagged or crooked the line.

I always wondered where Lorelei got her spark and her magic. It wasn't until after she was gone, while standing in a Budgie bird sanctuary with hundreds of colorful birds swarming me, that it clicked: Lorelei is a tiny version of me. Benji is a tiny version of Michael.

As rainbow feathers brushed my face and birds chirped all around, I laughed in delight while Michael and Benji recoiled in equal parts anxiety and disgust. In the midst of the feathery chaos, I thought about how much Lorelei would have loved it. She would have been shrieking with delight by my side, while the boys plotted their escape route.

For years I only saw her magic and light in moments like this, imagining how she would have lit up with joy, without ever realizing it was my joy too.

Lorelei's spark wasn't random—it was mine, reflected back. She was showing me who I was all along, the woman who could laugh in chaos, find magic in the ordinary, and finally believe she belonged in her own story.

Some days I roll my eyes at her for leaving me here with these two serious bears, but the truth is, she left me with proof of who I truly am. She left me with the confidence to finally believe I belonged in my own story, and the courage to keep turning the page.

Back in that NICU conference room when I was told my

daughter would never walk, never talk, or never eat by mouth, I thought it meant she wouldn't have a life to live, or a story to tell. But she did.

That's the gift of Lorelei's story—it isn't about a life cut short, or mitochondrial disease, or hospital visits, or pain. Her story is about love and faith and joy and magic and sunshine. It is about teaching me, and everyone who knows her, how to live fully in the chapters we are given.

I pray Lorelei and Benji are never "just a chapter" in my life story. They are my whole heart, and not a passing moment. Sometimes I picture myself as an old woman in a nursing home, memories slipping, framed photos on the nightstand. A nurse points to the pictures and asks if they're my grandchildren. But they're not. They're my children—my joy, my grief, my everything, all those years later. I never want my life to exist without their love, their humor, or their quirks woven through it.

That's the beautiful contradiction of it all: chapters may end, but some lives don't stay confined to one. They thread themselves through every page, binding the spine of the whole book.

They become the ink itself, the reason the words exist. Even when the storyline shifts, their presence shapes the meaning, reminding us that love doesn't just live in a single chapter; it lives in the entire narrative.

I started writing this book two months after Lorelei died. Back then, I thought I had already learned everything I could from her. I thought the story was finished. But stories like hers never really end—they echo, they ripple, they keep teaching.

Years later, as I finish this—the last chapter of my story *for now*—I can see it differently. Grief and time have weathered my jagged edges like sea glass, smoothed me in places, and deepened my perspective.

Lorelei still teaches me, even from beyond. She's taught me how to live like her, while not just telling her story, but carrying it forward. Now, with all the heartbreak and hope that's shaped these pages, I can finally say this is a book I am proud of. A story I am proud of. A life I am proud of.

To *Live Like Lorelei* is to write a story worth telling—hers and mine, braided together forever.

Epilogue

The Old Captain, Her Compass, Her Lantern

O nce upon a much later time, there was a 77-year-old woman with silver hair and pink highlights, wrinkled laugh lines, jaded tear lines, and paint under her fingernails she never bothered to scrub out. Along with her husband, she lived in a crooked little weathered house with an aqua front door in the Florida Keys that they probably couldn't afford, but also kept a camper van parked out front, just in case the wind whispered that it was time to roam.

Some days she was barefoot on the porch, stringing sea glass into wind chimes. Other days, she was driving backroads with the windows down, salty air tangling in her hair, singing off-key to songs from the 2000s like they were ancient hymns.

That old woman is me. And here's the thing: life didn't turn out like the storybook I once thought I was writing. It was messier. Harder. Far more heartbreaking. And yet, somehow, softer, brighter, and more beautiful too.

I still carry Lorelei's compass in my pocket, pointing me toward hope no matter how many storms I face. And on the dash of my van sits Benji's lantern, glowing with a steady light, reminding me I never travel alone. Between the compass and the lantern, I have never been lost, not really. Not even in the darkest nights.

So if you're reading this decades behind me, let me hand you what my children handed me: permission.

Permission to pivot, to change your mind, to start over, to take detours that don't make sense to anyone else. Straight lines are boring anyway. It's the curves, the swerves, the pivots, and the reroutes that make the story worth telling. Smooth seas never made a skilled sailor—and trust me, I've been tossed by enough storms to know that every choppy chapter has its place.

Consider this aged version of me giving the younger you a wide, open space to grow into yourself, while still having what you need to survive the plot twists.

Maybe your pivot is finally drawing boundaries where there never were any. Maybe it's divorce, illness, or infertility. Maybe it's the death of someone you love, or a quieter grief no one else can see. Maybe you're standing at the edge of a new season, terrified to turn the page.

But please hear me when I say this: you are not failing. You are not broken. You are not lost. You're simply in a chapter—and chapters change as stories evolve.

I didn't become a queen or a pirate. I became something better: a grandmother-without-grandkids, the kind who collects strays and dreamers, the kind who feeds the neighbors rum cake and tells them the truth when no one else will. The kind of old woman who knows that living is not about perfection, but about presence.

So pour yourself something good—at my age, I recommend tea with a splash of bourbon—and remember this: you don't need a polished map. Just a compass, a lantern, the salty air on your face, and the courage to keep telling your story. I'll be here, rocking on my porch swing, cheering you on and saving you a seat.

The rest of the story is yours now. Go live it.

With hope and stubborn joy –

Lorelei + Benji's Mama,

SUZ

♡

Lorelei's Eulogy

"Lessons From Lorelei"
written as I read it on July 20, 2021.

Listen to me—the author, the mama—reading it
at: www.suzgeoghegan.com/lorelei

Once upon a time... ha.

No for real though. I want to tell you all a story of a little girl. A little girl who had the odds stacked against her. Who was nonverbal. Who couldn't walk or crawl. Who was the 31st documented case of FBXL4 Mitochondrial Disease in the WORLD.

A little girl who changed that world.

Lorelei, oh sweet and fickle, beautiful and pure Lorelei. I would be lying if I said that throughout this almost 5 and a half year journey I didn't struggle with the thought that my kid didn't have friends. We were rarely anywhere but home, hospitals and doctor offices. But here we are, in a ballroom with a waterfront view, full of people, some of you strangers, who my five-year-old impacted.

The night after Lorelei's passing, I found myself saying, "I can't do this. I don't want this. This isn't my plan. I cannot do this." As I repeated these thoughts over and over, I froze, realizing I have said these words before. Many, many times, but especially early in our journey as a rare disease family.

And you know what, maybe it wasn't my plan, but I did it. We all did it.

And we did it well.

At one point in this adventure, I found myself googling "nearest children's hospital" in Orlando, Florida and rushing Lorelei to it. A bewildered resident in the ED dropped the ultimate F Bomb: Lorelei had the flu. The ICU attending at the time came down to the ED and sat across from me, everyone knowing how grim this situation could be for an almost-two year old with Mitochondrial Disease.

He said, "So tell me about Lorelei." I immediately jumped into her medical history, how we needed VAT, the labs that needed to be run, how we—he stopped me. He said, "no, tell me about Lorelei." I paused in a moment of confusion. He said "What does she like? Who is she?"

So today, y'all, today I am going to tell you about Lorelei. Who she was and who she will always be. I'm going to share things I learned from her, beyond the fact that the mitochondria is the powerhouse of your cells.

Here are 15 Lessons from Lorelei.

Lesson Number One: Do not take your calendar too seriously.

The child arrived two months early. She caused us to cancel and rearrange countless vacations and camping trips. She never hit milestones on time. She loved her CHKD family so much she spent 75% of her admissions and ED visits there on holidays.

As someone who thrived and functioned with plans and a calendar written in ink prior to Lorelei... I may have fought it and hated it every step of the way, but at some point I realized that sometimes plans just don't happen. Events can be skipped. Vacations can be redone. Holidays can be celebrated on other days.

Lesson Number Two: Be outside as much as possible.

Appreciate the breeze on your face. Feel it, laugh at your hair blowing in your eye lashes. Be present with the temperature of the air and the energy the sun gives you. Feel the grass and take in the prickly texture. Tweeting birds are adorable and hilarious. Camping is the best escape.

And if you cannot be outside, find a view. Lorelei struggled to regulate her body temperature so when it was too hot, too humid or simply raining outside, you would often find her sitting in her chair like a little old lady, looking out the window. The last month of her life, Make a Wish and Ferguson Building Corporation made Lorelei's wish come true. She wished to be outside, but inside. They built her an amazing She Shed called Fort Lorelei that has windows all the way around it. While she was only able to use this space

213

for a few weeks, it was a magical way for her to enjoy her last bit of summer.

Lesson Number Three: Dance every day.

Even if you are a terrible dancer. Even if your body won't physically allow you to dance. Wiggle your toes, kick your feet, bobble your head, blast some music and dance. It is good for your soul.

Lesson Number Four: Communication comes in all forms.

People often ask me "how do you know what your children need or want?" To be quite frank, I have no clue. I just know. I knew Lorelei better than any human on this planet. I knew her needs and when she was going to puke. I knew what emotion she was feeling. I just knew. But Lorelei communicated with everyone else in different ways. You just had to pause for a minute to catch it...

Lorelei had what we lovingly called "The Resting Mito Face" and just like the "RBF" it spoke volumes. She would clap her hands for yes or no questions. She would look in the direction of something she wanted.

In the last couple years of her life, we were paired up with a Speech Therapist who pushed my kid. She loved her but she pushed her. And Lorelei was able to use a communication computer that we call "her tobii talker". When she was feeling like talking (because let's be real sometimes we just don't want to talk) Lorelei would use her eyes to push buttons on the screen.

Every time she was able to answer Yes or No questions, my heart exploded. The first time we got into an argument with each other, my heart exploded. When Speech therapy would start and Lorelei would immediately say "I want. All done." Ms Cat would be firm but I know her heart was exploding too. When we were in the PICU, after a long, long day, Chaplain Anne walked in to visit us and Lorelei said "I want. All done. Goodbye. All done. Goodbye. All done. Goodbye." We laughed and collectively, all of our hearts exploded.

When she was able to say "I love you" for the first time with the help of her tobii... my heart absolutely exploded with confetti and glitter all over my kitchen floor.

Far from traditional communication but if we learned anything from Lorelei it's that we need to meet people where they are, take a minute and let them get their message out, however they need to do it, whenever they need to do it, because beautiful things can happen.

Lesson Number Five: A hammock is never, ever a bad idea.

Lesson Number Six: You do not have to say or do a lot, or even leave your house, to make an impact.

I kinda want to channel Lorelei's sass right now and say "Lorelei was five and nonverbal, what's your excuse?"

There are so many dark things in our world, in this society, in the environment right now. But we can still do good. So much good. Lorelei had a way about her, a way that sucked people in and pushed them to be better humans. With Lorelei, because of Lorelei, we raised awareness and money for Mitochondrial Disease that led to trial medications (one of which Benji was able to use on day one of his life!). We had book drives for the NICU. We volunteered at the

Ronald McDonald House, feeding families who were going through their worst days ever. We Floated for a Mito Cure. Our family taught new doctors what life is like as a medical family. I volunteered with brand spankin' new medical moms in the NICU. Because of Lorelei and this life, I started a podcast to help mamas and the people who love them navigate a hard life they didn't expect to be living.

I believe it was Mr Feeny in the finale of the classic 90s show Boy Meets World who said, "Do good." Topanga said, "Don't you mean 'Do well?'" Feeny said "No. Do Good."

When Michael and I were handed a beautiful little red headed baby with a grim and dark prognosis, we made a commitment that our family would "Do good." And Lorelei did.

Lesson Number Seven: Do not take life too seriously. None of us make it out alive.

If I'm being quite real, Lorelei probably had more bad days than anyone wants to admit. Science said she had a two to five year life expectancy. She dealt with more medical treatments and procedures than most of us in this room with ever face. But that never stopped her from laughing at fart noises, squawking with joy when she was surrounded by love, and clapping her hands because she was happy, and she knew it. Sometimes things are not fair and they suck, a lot. But when so much was wrong, Lorelei chose joy and laughter.

Lesson Number Eight: Water. Is. Life.

Puke all over yourself so your mama will be forced to give you multiple baths a day if that's what it takes to be in the bathtub!

But for real though: Water is good for the soul. Splash in it. Play in it. Float in it.

Lesson Number Nine: Embrace what you are handed.

Crazy hair and a "Dilustro do?" Rock it.

Life threatening disease? Prove them wrong and live it up.

Poor muscle tone preventing you from walking? Rolling across the room will also get you up under that Christmas tree. Just because you "can't do something" doesn't mean there isn't another way.

Lesson Number Ten: Make a list.

On the day Lorelei was born, God knew when he would be calling her home. But I didn't. So I tried to make the most of the time I was going to have with my daughter by creating a bucket list. An amazing, marvelous bucket list that led us to so many great things:

· catching a baseball at a Tides game,

· meeting the JMU duke dog

· going to Disney world, almost dying and then redoing Disney world so she could stand with Mickey Mouse and show Anna and Elsa that Lorelei was a real princess just like them

· boat rides with Grandma and Papa B

· taking a ballet class with Ms Meredith

· getting a goldendoodle companion pup

· having her dada walk her down the aisle as the flower girl for her Auntie and Uncle Mister's wedding

· a pony party in our backyard

· becoming a Girl Scout, selling almost 800 boxes of

cookies and giving them to her CHKD family, and going to Girl Scout camp

I know I'm missing things, but the point is, none of us know how all of this is going to play out. I know we all have bills to pay and jobs to do, but are you making the most of your time here? I think we all owe it to Lorelei to check something off our own bucket lists this summer.

Lesson Number Eleven: Compliment people and let them know they are loved.

You don't even have to do it with your words. Remember communication comes in all forms. But if you love something about someone, let them know. If you are digging someone's beard and hat (I'm looking at you Uncle Mister and Santa Claus) make sure they know it. Smile when you see your loved ones. "Mmmmm" if something hits your heart just right. Cuddle. Facetime. Connect with your friends and family every chance you get.

Lesson Number Twelve: You do not have to eat everything that is put in front of you.

But you should always, ALWAYS lick the guacamole and ranch dressing.

Lesson Number Thirteen: When things get hard, look up.

Scratch that. Always, look up. And I'm not saying this because she spent a lot of time laying on her back on the living room floor... I'm saying this because there is a higher plan. We all felt it and we all knew it from Day One of Lorelei's life.

Lorelei trusted. She trusted God and the universe,

strangers in the hospital, and her mama and dada when things were bad. She never ever, ever stopped trusting.

Lesson Number Fourteen: It is okay to be rare and different.

Let me say that again for the people out on the deck. It is soooo okay to be rare and different. I mean, I'm sure her doctors may disagree to a point because Lorelei followed ZERO medical rules, making us feel like we are throwing things at the wall until we found something that stuck... but rare is good. Rare is unique. Rare is beautiful. Rare makes this life and our community diverse, amazing, and far from boring.

Lesson Number Fifteen: Read before bed.

I'm still trying with this one. Because by the time I'm ready to go to bed, my brain is tired and all I want to do is curl up and sleep. But Lorelei was a big fan of cuddles and bedtime stories. We would snuggle up together every night, she would pick the book (which let me tell you, she always picked the book in my left hand so when I was super tired you better believe the book with a mere 5 words was the one on the left...) Most nights though, our favorite to read together was "On the Night You Were Born." For years Michael and I read it to her. And almost every time I read it I thought, one day I will share this at your funeral. So if you don't mind, I am going to wrap this up with reading our favorite bedtime story:

READ *"On the Night You Were Born"* by Nancy Tillman

I want to end with a quote that my co-hostess on my

podcast references all the time – "Together at the same time without blending the two."

It's okay to feel sad in this moment while you are rejoicing at the same time. It's okay to feel an ache and emptiness in your core but also feel like you can breathe and that your heart is full of love.

Acknowledge your worries but feel hope, always.

Lorelei's life and death were tragically beautiful and I am so incredibly grateful God chose me to be a part of her story.

Coffee • Conversation

At the Apricity Hideaway, we always make space for Coffee + Convo Sessions—time carved out for honesty, reflection, and connection. Think of this section as your own personal retreat: grab a journal, pour something delicious into your favorite mug, and settle in.

These questions are here for *you*. Use them as private journal prompts, quiet reflections on a walk, or as conversation starters if you're gathering with friends, a book club, or your own little flock. There's no right or wrong way to do this —just an invitation to sit with the story you've just read and notice how it stirs your own.

Part One: Before Lorelei

- What expectations did you once hold for your own life, and how have they shifted?

- When has life taken you somewhere completely different than you planned?
- What role does intuition or "the little voice inside" play in your story?

Part Two: With Lorelei

- What moments of unexpected joy or laughter carried you through your own hard seasons?
- Have you ever found yourself stronger or more resilient than you thought possible?
- How do you define "advocacy" in your own life— who or what do you fight for?
- When have you experienced connection without words?
- Have you ever felt angry at God (or the universe)? What did you do with that anger?
- What does surrendering control look like for you? When has it felt freeing, and when has it felt impossible?

Part Three: After Lorelei

- What have you carried forward from someone you've lost—or from a hard chapter of your life?
- How do you honor both grief and gratitude at the same time?
- What does "hope" look like to you right now—not in a polished sense, but in the messy, everyday kind of way?

- Is there a sign, symbol, or moment you use to feel connected with loved ones on the other side?
- How do you want your story to ripple into the lives of others?

Live Like Lorelei

- How has this book challenged the way you think about what makes a life "beautiful" or "successful"?
- Where do you see the tension between control and surrender in your own story?
- What does resilience mean to you now—after walking through this book—compared to before?
- How can you bring more kindness (to yourself and to others) into the messy, ordinary days?
- What does "living like Lorelei" mean to you?

For a full Book Club Conversation Guide and more resources, please visit www.suzgeoghegan.com.

Appendix 1

For Grievers: Tiny Pressure Valves & What Helped Me

When I say *griever,* I don't just mean someone dressed in black at a funeral. A griever is anyone waking up in a life they didn't plan for: medical moms, caregivers, anyone quietly mourning the "supposed to be" version of their story. Grievers are people who have lost something they can't get back—a person, a plan, or a version of life that once felt promised.

Grief is a beast. It doesn't follow rules, it doesn't care about your calendar, and it certainly doesn't clean up after itself. I can't tell you what will "fix" it (spoiler: nothing will), but I can share the things that kept me breathing when the weight felt unbearable—and the things that most definitely did not.

What Helped Me

- **Therapy.** A place to be messy without judgment—if you find the right fit. Ask upfront if they can handle your kind of grief and give you tools to carry outside their office.

- **Using Lorelei's name.** Saying it, hearing it, writing it—keeping her close and present.

- **Friends who showed up quietly.** The ones who texted "coffee's on the porch" or "drink your water" instead of "let me know if you need anything."

- **Permission to say no.** To events, to people, to "shoulds."

- **Sarcasm.** Humor that cracked open little air pockets when the grief got too suffocating. Also my subliminal way of saying "fuck mito."

- **Nature.** Sunsets, apricity, salty air, long walks, sandbars. The earth tending grief in quiet, steady ways.

- **Art + creativity.** Painting, journaling, messy crafts, rearranging words on a page. Grief needed somewhere to go.

- **Small comforts.** Good coffee, soft blankets, pie, and playlists that let me cry just enough.

What Didn't Help

- **Platitudes.** ("Everything happens for a reason." "Special parents for special needs kids." Hard pass.)

- **People who vanished.** Disappearing friends hurt almost as much as the loss.

- **Toxic positivity.** Pretending everything was fine made me feel worse. We don't have to find the silver lining in loss.

- **Pressure to "move on."** Grief doesn't pack up neatly after 30 days.

- **Feeling like I had to be strong.** For once, strength wasn't the point. Survival was.

Tiny Pressure Valves

Sometimes grief needs an outlet—little steam releases to keep the whole thing from exploding. Here are mine:

- Crying in the shower where no one could hear me

- Trash TV marathons (I owe Bravo TV my sanity)

- Candy Crush (I may or may not be on level 6577)

- Dark humor with fellow grievers

- Car karaoke with the windows up

- Doodling, coloring, or scribbling all over a calendar

- Coffee. Always coffee.

- Pie. Always key lime.

There's no "right way" to grieve. If you're in it, I see you. If all you do today is breathe and find one tiny valve to let out the steam, that's enough.

Appendix 2

For Friends of Grievers: Tiny Pressure Valves & How to Show Up in Hard Seasons

Grief isn't just about funerals. It shows up in hospital rooms, in empty bedrooms, in "supposed to be" lives that look nothing like the plan. It doesn't follow a timeline, come with a handbook, or end when the casseroles stop arriving.

If you love someone walking through one of these hard seasons, it's less about having the perfect words and more about being the person who sticks around when things get uncomfortable. And when I say *friend*, I don't just mean your bestie who knows your Starbucks order. I mean anyone who chooses to show up—neighbors, coworkers, in-laws, church people, podcast listeners. If you're in their orbit and you care, you can be a "friend" in grief.

What Helps

- **Show up without fixing.** You don't need to solve it—you just need to be there.

- **Simple texts.** "Thinking of you. No need to reply." (Yes, send it even if you feel awkward.)

- **Practical help.** "I'm at Target—want me to grab paper towels?" always beats "let me know if you need anything."

- **Consistent presence.** Keep inviting them, even if they say no ten times. (Spoiler: eventually, one of those invites will land.)

- **Remember the dates.** Birthdays, anniversaries, diagnosis days, death days. Put them in your phone like you'd put in a dentist appointment.

- **Use their person's name.** You're not reminding us of their absence; you're honoring their presence.

- **Food + coffee.** Always welcome. Bonus points

if you drop caffeine on the porch and don't ring the doorbell.

What Hurts

- **Disappearing.** Don't ghost after two weeks. Grief is a marathon, not a sprint.

- **Platitudes.** "At least they're no longer in pain." Just... no. Hard pass.

- **Comparisons.** "When my dog died..." is not it. (Unless your dog was on a ventilator in the PICU. Which he wasn't.)

- **Timelines.** Don't hint that anyone should be "better by now."

- **Toxic cheerleading.** Grief isn't cured by a "just stay positive!" pep talk.

- **Emotional dumping.** Don't unload your fear, sadness, or "I just can't imagine" speech on the griever. That weight belongs with your therapist, your spouse, or a friend further removed—not the person already carrying the heaviest load.

Practical Ways to Stay

- **Put reminders in your phone.** Siri and Google Calendar exist for a reason.

- **Offer specifics.** "I'll bring tacos Tuesday" > "Let me know if you need anything."

- **Sit in the silence.** Sometimes your presence speaks louder than your words.

- **Keep showing up.** Weeks, months, years later. Even a meme text counts.

- **Accept the awkward.** You won't always say the perfect thing. That's okay—awkward love is still love.

Tiny Pressure Valves (for Friends)

Sometimes grief needs an outlet—and sometimes you can help create one. Here are tiny ways to ease the pressure for the person you love:

- Deliver tacos + margaritas, no explanation needed.

- Text "drink water" or "take your meds" like a loving drill sergeant.

- Send a meme at midnight—laughter counts as medicine.

- Write their person's name in a card and mail it.

- Show up with cleaning supplies or groceries when life falls apart, not just flowers.

- Invite them over with zero expectation they'll say yes.

- Check in on the random Tuesday in November, not just the holidays.

There's no perfect script for showing up in grief. If all you do today is one small, imperfect thing—a text, a Chick-fil-A milkshake, a quiet presence—that's enough.

Appendix 3

Resources & Organizations: Where to Turn in Hard Seasons

Grief, caregiving, and life in the in-between can feel isolating —but you don't have to do it alone. These are a few of the organizations and voices that made a difference for me, and I hope they might do the same for you.

For a regularly updated, more detailed list of resources, please visit: **www.suzgeoghegan.com/resources**

Caregiving + Medical Parent Resources

- **The Apricity Hope Project** – Retreats, resources, and community for caregiving parents (yes, this is my nonprofit!).

- www.apricityhope.org

- **When Autumn Comes Podcast** – Stories of medical parenthood and caregiving, reminding you you're not alone.
  - www.apricityhope.org/autumn

- **United Mitochondrial Disease Foundation** – Education and advocacy for mito families.
  - www.umdf.org

- **MitoAction** – Support and resources for families impacted by mitochondrial disease.
  - www.mitoaction.org

- **Marty Lyons Foundation** – Wishes and support for children facing life-threatening illness.
  - www.martylyonsfoundation.org

- **Give Kids the World Village** – A magical, all-inclusive vacation village for children with critical illnesses.
  - www.gktw.org

- **Books by Abigail Gellene-Beaudoin** – Navigating hope and loss as a family.
  - www.abigailgellenebeaudoin.com

- ***How to Handle More Than You Can Handle* by Amanda Griffith-Atkins** – A book about caring for yourself while raising a disabled child.
  - www.amandagriffithatkins.com

- ***Breath Taking* by Jessica Fein** – A memoir for parents navigating love, loss, and living fully while caregiving.
  - www.jessicafeinstories.com

- **The Disorder Channel** – A streaming platform sharing rare disease stories from around the world.
  - www.thedisordercollection.com

- **Global Genes** – Resources and connections for rare disease families.
  - www.globalgenes.org

Grief + Loss Support

- **Jeni Juranics** – International evidential medium and psychic.
  - www.jenijuranics.com

- **Helping Parents Heal** – Peer support for parents after child loss.
  - www.helpingparentsheal.org

- **Hayden's House of Healing** – Retreats and programs for bereaved families.
  - www.haydenshouse.org

- **Books by Laura Lynne Jackson** – Exploring connection, love, and life after loss.
  - www.lauralynnejackson.com

This is not an exhaustive list—just a beginning. Pick what feels right, skip what doesn't. And for more resources, updated regularly, visit:

www.suzgeoghegan.com/resources.

The point is simple: you don't have to carry it alone.

Acknowledgments

I've written more words than I ever thought I could, but I can't end this without thanking a few important characters in my story:

Thank you Lorelei and Benji, for picking me to be your mama.

Thank you Michael, for taking this journey with me—and for the hungry chicken.

To my mom, Ruth, for always being my biggest fan and pushing me to reach for the stars.

To my dad, Alan, for passing down a signature sense of sarcasm that's gotten me here today.

To my sister, Leslie, who is my opposite and my twin, and who loves my kids with her whole heart.

To Aaron, for being Uncle Mister with a beard, and for making me mai tais.

To my godmothers, Jean and Lou, for proving that chosen family comes with sarcasm and sanctuary.

To my Golden Girls, Christen and Amanda, for being the most supportive friends I've ever had.

To Caitlin, for decades of friendship and reality television.

To Jess, for always swooping for the during tough times, often with pina coladas.

To our incredible team of nurses and doctors, with an honorable mention to: Dr. Moukalled, Dr. Vergano, Dr. Cummings, Dr. Khan, Dr. Foley—but especially Dr. Ami Mehta, from the NICU to the PICU, who always cared for our family as a whole and has been our "Dr. House" when things got too rare.

To Ms. Cat, who is better than Ms. Rachel.

To Diane and Katrina, my podcast partners in crime and paradox.

To Norway, Gunhild, and Nea, for our soul-sisterhood.

To Alex, and the #DeadKidCon.

To Katherine, for the nonstop love winks.

To Jeni, for rainbows and bald men.

To Jenna, for kidnapping me, and for saving her life.

To Anne, and to Snoop Dog, for prayers and curse words.

To Reagan, for being Benji's bestie, my life raft and for finding my unfinished manuscript and forcing me to write.

To Sinead, for memes, numbers and showing up.

To Christi, for knowing where my phone is and for taking care of me when I'm old.

To Abbey, for breaking walls and cleaning up after Roberta.

To Amy, for piles of pie.

To Keri-Lyn, for giving Lorelei a lab coat.

To Ally, for sandbars and manatees.

To John, for sarcasm with a side of trauma therapy.

To Josh, for being a pinch hitter editor despite my salt.

To Euffie, for printables and brain-dumping.

To Jovie Doodle and Ollie Collie, for your velcro love and compulsive herding.

To the When Autumn Comes and Fridays With Lorelei communities, for supporting, encouraging and humoring my storytelling.

To the AHP Board, for helping me build a pink table big enough for all of us.

To the Mingos, for believing in me and for building this community by my side.

And to you, reading this—if you laughed, cried, or snorted coffee out your nose, then my job here is done. Thanks for letting me dump my soul onto these pages. Next round of grief pie is on me.

About the Author

Susan B. Geoghegan is a writer, speaker, podcaster, grief artist, and—most importantly—mama. She's been known to mix sarcasm with stubborn hope, because sometimes the only way through the storm is with equal parts humor and heart. Whether she's on a TEDx stage, behind a microphone on the *When Autumn Comes* podcast, leading retreats at the Apricity Hideaway, or covered in paint in Lorelei's She Shed,

Susan creates spaces where grief and joy are allowed to sit side by side. She also believes sunsets, salt water, and the occasional piña colada are sacred medicine for the soul.

She is the founder of *The Apricity Hope Project* and HOPE FULL Co. She lives in Virginia with her husband, Michael, their son, Benji, their pups Jovie Doodle and Ollie Collie— and with the memory of her daughter, Lorelei, whose sparkle still shows up in rainbows and hearts all around their home.

Learn more or connect with Susan at www.suzgeoghe-gan.com.

About The Apricity Hope Project

The Apricity Hope Project was built on one truth: caregivers matter too. And in order to care for children fighting big battles, we must care for the parents as well. Founded in honor of past versions of herself—especially the new, scared mom sitting in the NICU—the nonprofit gives parents of disabled and medically complex children a chance to exhale and feel seen. Through retreats, hospital go-bags, the *When Autumn Comes* podcast, and community programs, The Apricity Hope Project offers more than rest; it helps caregivers find their light again, even when life feels impossibly heavy.

Learn more or join the flock at www.apricityhope.org.

Also by Susan B. Geoghegan

A companion to *Live Like Lorelei*, this children's book brings Lorelei's sparkle to life in whimsical watercolor illustrations and simple truths meant for the whole family.

Just as this memoir invites you into the lessons Lorelei left behind, *How to Live Like Lorelei* offers those same lessons, or as Lorelei calls them, "secrets", in a way children can hold onto—rainbows, hearts, and hope included.